The
POINT-TO-POINT
Recruits 2019/20

Jodie Standing

Published by
Marten Julian
69 Highgate, Kendal,
Cumbria, LA9 4ED
01539 741 007

rebecca@martenjulian.com
www.martenjulian.com

Marten Julian (Publisher)
69 Highgate, Kendal, Cumbria LA9 4ED
www.martenjulian.com

MARTEN
JULIAN

1970 • 2019

First published in Great Britain in 2019

Copyright © Jodie Standing

ISBN: 978-1-9162387-2-5

ISSN: 2633-2418 (Print)

Book Design & Layout
Steve Dixon

Cover/Book Photographs
Susie Cahill
Email: susiecahill@gmail.com

Thank you for purchasing this second edition of *The Point-To-Point Recruits*. I hope that you find this book a useful source of reference for the coming season and beyond.

The point-to-point footage and form is not the most accessible and many of you will be seeing these horses for the first time when they hit the track. With this book, I am trying to shed some light on a horse's performance and their characteristics before they run in the hope that it may give us a slight edge and earn us some profit along the way.

I have expressed my opinion on 94 lightly raced individuals from the British and Irish pointing fields which, in my view, possess the ability to make an impact for their new connections. Amongst those horses mentioned are a special 25 which, I believe, have 'star' potential. This does not necessarily mean I believe they will all reach the highest level, but I expect them to do especially well for their new connections.

It has always been a passion of mine to spot early talent. Throughout my life I have been involved in the early stages of development, whether it has been with the animals on the Cumbrian farm where I grew up or teaching children to hit their first tennis ball in my days as a tennis coach. The fundamentals are the same and there is nothing more satisfying than to see potential realised that you first saw at the beginning.

The writing of this book has been extremely enjoyable while also, at times, being somewhat absorbing. I would like to take this opportunity to thank Marten Julian for being a big support to me. I am also indebted to Rebecca Julian-Dixon, Steve Dixon, Ian Greensill, Alessandro Claus and everyone who took time to answer my queries at various stages along the way.

A special thank you must go to Susie Cahill for providing all the wonderful photos for this book, including the front cover. To view more of her talented work, please refer to *Page 4.*

Finally, it just leaves me to say that I hope everyone has a successful and enjoyable National Hunt season.

Best wishes

Jodie Standing

The following horses have all shown sufficient ability or potential to suggest they can make an impact under Rules for their new connections. As is the case with any horse, they will thrive at different stages of their careers. It may take time before some of them fulfil their potential while others may be precocious enough to win bumpers and novice hurdles this season.

Beaten in Bumper 16m ?

ADRIMEL
4YR BAY/BROWN GELDING

TRAINER:	Tom Lacey
PEDIGREE:	Tirwanako – Irise De Gene (Blushing Flame)
FORM (P2P):	1
OPTIMUM TRIP:	2m +
GOING:	Soft

★ STAR POTENTIAL ★

Adrimel looked an ultra-professional type as he produced a polished round of jumping en route to success at Ballyarthur in March.

The four-year-old barely saw his opposition as he helped set the early pace and jumped into a clear lead at the fifth from home. Not for hanging around, he pressed on to hold a commanding advantage at the next and his jockey, James Hannon, stole a look over his shoulder before injecting a little more pace.

With ears pricked, the gelding continued to stride on, and his dominance grew further with the departure of his nearest pursuer at the third from home, leaving only the ridden along Firak to try and bridge the gap. He managed to get within three lengths on the run to the penultimate fence but a spring-heeled leap from this gelding saw him land with momentum which propelled him further clear as they galloped to the last. Still on the bridle, he was allowed to run down the fence and although he landed untidily, he soon regathered his stride before going on to win by an eased-down eight lengths.

I liked the way Adrimel went through the race. He was eager without being keen and appeared to relish the challenge of the fences. He spied them a couple of strides out and although he got his timing wrong at a couple – mostly in the latter stages which could be due to fatigue – he made a lovely shape in the air.

Trained by Joe Ryan, the gelding was purchased by his son Josh as a three-year-old store at the Tattersalls August Sale for a mere €11,000 and got a hefty return for his money when he went through the ring earlier this year at Aintree for £280,000 selling to Ed Bailey Bloodstock who was standing alongside Tom Lacey.

He had plenty of presence as he paraded around the sales ring. He's a big imposing sort with a lovely loose walk and a relaxed sort of demeanour. Probably the pick of the sale for me.

Tirwanako is a sire we don't hear much about, but of the five runners he has sired in the UK, four have won – three of which attained marks in the 140s. This gelding is a half-brother to 2m5f French Chase winner Gus De Gene out of an unraced half-sister to Welsh National winner Halcon Genelardais.

He showed plenty of speed in his point which could see him able to line up in bumpers but given his back pedigree and natural ability over fences, he should develop into a fantastic chaser.

ASK A HONEY BEE
5YR BAY GELDING

TRAINER:	Fergal O'Brien
PEDIGREE:	Ask – Pure Honey (Beneficial)
FORM (P2P):	3341 -
OPTIMUM TRIP:	3m +
GOING:	Good

Fairly exposed between the flags, but tremendously game and sure to have more to offer under Rules.

Ask A Honey Bee showed distinct ability when responding well to finish an eye-catching third on his debut in a hotly contested maiden at Dungarvan in January won by the well-regarded Getaway Pat. He then filled the same position at Knockanard the following month, before finishing a six-and-a-half-length fourth at Lismore where he rallied gamely before tiring in testing conditions.

Finally off the mark at Ballynoe at the end of March, he travelled kindly on the heels of the leaders before being cajoled after the third from home. Despite dropping to fourth position, he fought back tenaciously and challenged for the lead at the penultimate fence before pulling out extra in the dying strides to win by one and a half lengths.

The form has a strong look to it. Cape Robin, who was over 16 lengths back in fourth, went on to win his next start and has since been purchased by Tim Vaughan for £10,000. The fifth also won on his next outing and was purchased for £19,000 by Nick Kent and Stuart Parkin at Doncaster in May, whilst the favourite, Epalo De La Thinte, was a head second on his next start.

Ask A Honey Bee is a half-brother to point winner Baby Bee. His dam is an unraced sister to point and 2m hurdle winner Gold Cygnet, and also a half-sister to bumper/2m6f-3m hurdle/chase winner Wind Instrument.

Bought for £38,000 at the Goffs Sale at Doncaster in May by Fergal O'Brien.

He looks a progressive sort and one which his trainer should be able to place to great effect. His game attitude is an asset to him.

BALLINSKER
4YR BAY GELDING

TRAINER:	Evan Williams
PEDIGREE:	Court Cave – Brownie Points (Bob Back)
FORM (P2P):	1 -
OPTIMUM TRIP:	2m +
GOING:	Good

Ballinsker showed a thoroughly likeable attitude on his debut at Oldcastle to follow in the footsteps of Cenotice who won the race 12 months ago for the same connections.

Trained by Michael Goff and ridden by Shane Fitzgerald, the good-looking son of Court Cave always moved well in a share of the lead before upping the pace as he pressed on over the fifth from home. He continued out in front with a two-length lead over the next and still travelled kindly on the approach to the third last where he was almost joined on his outside.

Ridden to reassert his advantage on the run to the penultimate fence, the gelding saw a good stride and jumped well before marching on with purpose around the bend for home. Stretching clear by the best part of six lengths as he reached the last, he popped over nicely and sauntered up the run-in for an easy eight-length success from Belfast Banter, who has since gone on to win a bumper for Dan Skelton by seven lengths.

Purchased by Evan Williams for £90,000 at the Tattersalls Sale at Cheltenham in April.

Ballinsker is a half-brother to Tardree who placed in a point-to-point last season. His dam achieved very little but is a half-sister to bumper/2m hurdle/2m1f chase winner Gee Hi and 2m hurdle winner Estuary Princess out of a maiden sister to 1m-1m4f Group 1 winner In The Groove.

By Court Cave, I would expect the four-year-old to be mostly at home on good ground. He also has plenty of speed and maybe one to look out for in an early-season bumper.

Runners taking three from home at the picturesque Oldcastle

BAPTISM OF FIRE
4YR BAY GELDING

TRAINER:	TBC
PEDIGREE:	Jeremy – Julia Glynn (Bob's Return)
FORM (P2P):	1 -
OPTIMUM TRIP:	2m +
GOING:	Good to Soft

Jamie Codd deserved ride of the season when getting Baptism Of Fire up in the shadows of the post.

The €48,000 store purchase made his debut in a four-year-olds' maiden at Courtown in April and was sent off the 6/4 favourite for trainer Denis Murphy.

The bay appeared to travel well in the soft conditions but lost his pitch when the pace increased at the fourth from home and dropped to sixth position. Nudged along on the uphill run to the next, he recovered a little of the lost ground and moved back into fourth place but was still around seven lengths adrift of the leading trio.

Firmly ridden after jumping the penultimate fence, victory looked out of the question, but the penny appeared to drop on the long run to the last where he moved into third place before quickening and jumping the fence in his stride. With momentum firmly in his favour he managed to bridge the four-length deficit and snatch victory in the dying strides from Colin Bowe's Tupelo Mississippi.

Denis Murphy said following the race, "He probably looked a little too well in the ring. Another couple of weeks wouldn't have gone astray on him but he just rattled home. His work was unreal; you'll hear a lot about this lad."

The runner-up was subsequently purchased by Phil Green for £65,000 whilst the third, who looked the likely winner jumping the last, is now in the care of Donald McCain after being purchased for £37,000. This gelding cost quite a bit more when selling for £100,000 at Cheltenham in April to Margaret O'Toole.

His dam is an unraced half-sister to bumper/2m4f-3m1f hurdle/smart chase winner Casey Jones, 2m6f hurdle winner Carheenlea, 2m chase winner Dante's Brook and 3m chase winner The Rebel Lady.

With experience under his belt, there certainly looks more to come from this exciting sort, especially over a shorter trip on some better ground.

BARBADOS BUCK'S
4YR BAY GELDING

TRAINER:	Paul Nicholls
PEDIGREE:	Getaway – Buck's Blue (Epervier Bleu)
FORM (P2P):	2 -
OPTIMUM TRIP:	2m 4f +
GOING:	Soft

Barbados Buck's comes from a family Paul Nicholls knows exceptionally well and has been purchased to run in the colours of Andy Stewart.

The supremely well-bred gelding is a half-brother to More Buck's who was successful in bumpers, hurdles and chases for the Ditcheat trainer, before winning the Listed Summer Plate at Market Rasen for Peter Bowen. He is also a full brother to Nicky Henderson's bumper/2m5f hurdle winner Barbados Blue and point winner Getabuck. His dam is a French 2m3f hurdle-winning half-sister to the outstanding staying hurdler Big Buck's.

Trained by Richard Black and ridden by Luke Murphy, the four-year-old made his debut in a strongly contested maiden at Dromahane towards the end of April where he tracked the leaders before trying to slip the field after a good jump at the fourth from home. He continued to lead by two lengths at the next but was slightly ponderous and looked a little lonely on the level before being joined at the penultimate fence by Skatman who touched down with a length advantage. Once given a few sharp reminders by his jockey, Barbados Buck's knuckled down well and was almost back alongside as the pair rose over the last but he lacked the change of gear on the short run to the line.

He was only beaten two lengths by Skatman who had th
five-pound claimer and Tom Malone acting on behalf of .
obviously rates the form as not only did he buy this gelding
the Goffs Punchestown Sale in May, he was also responsibl
winner a few weeks later at Doncaster for £170,000.

Getaway produces stock which can go on any ground, but this ,
be more effective on a softer surface than he encountered at Dro. ...ane.
He should also possess enough speed for bumpers this season.

HASN'T RUN YET

BELLA BALLERINA
5YR BAY MARE

TRAINER:	TBC
PEDIGREE:	Yeats – The Real Athlete (Presenting)
FORM (P2P):	3 - 1
OPTIMUM TRIP:	2m +
GOING:	Soft

★ **STAR POTENTIAL** ★

This mare has a potent turn of foot and looks certain of track success.

The well-related daughter of Yeats was a well-supported evens favourite
when making her debut under Derek O'Connor at Cragmore back in
February where she was given a patient ride towards the rear before making
steady progress through the field and being left in third position at the
penultimate fence.

Given plenty of time between runs, she reappeared towards the end of
April at Monksgrange where she rewarded her supporters in no uncertain
terms to return a very easy three-length winner from the subsequent eight-
length winner Mt Leinster Gold.

Ridden more prominently under Barry O'Neill, Bella Ballerina scythed her
way through the field on the approach to the fifth from home and touched
down in a share of the lead before continuing to hold her position over the
next two fences. Still hard on the bridle as the field climbed to the top of
the hill, she really began to motor on the descent towards the penultimate
fence and came up well before edging into a clear lead as she pricked her
ears on the run to the last. Ridden to see a stride, she responded with a big

...d quickened impressively upon touching down, readily asserting in a ...tter of strides without being asked any questions.

This was a hugely impressive victory where the winning margin could easily have been far greater if Barry O'Neill had wished.

By Yeats out of a Presenting mare, she is closely related to bumper/useful 2m4f-3m1f hurdle/chase winner Real Milan and point winner Milan Athlete. Her dam is an unraced half-sister to useful 2m4f hurdle/2m6f chase winner Get It Done with the further family linking back to Grand National winner Royal Athlete.

Bella Ballerina has plenty of stamina and an impressive turn of foot which should see her competitive over a range of trips. I loved how she kept upping the ante in the latter stages and always appeared at ease with herself.

She could be something special.

WON ITS FIRST HURDLE

BIG BRESIL
4YR BAY GELDING

TRAINER:	Tom George
PEDIGREE:	Blue Bresil – Cutielilou (Astarabad)
FORM (P2P):	2 -
OPTIMUM TRIP:	2m +
GOING:	Good to Soft

★ **STAR POTENTIAL** ★

Big Bresil showed plenty on his debut to suggest he can make an impact under Rules for his new connections.

The good-looking individual started his career in a four-year-olds' maiden at Liscarroll in March where he lost nothing in defeat when finishing second to Papa Tango Charly who subsequently sold for £440,000 at the Aintree Sale in April.

Having forced the pace from the drop of the flag, the gelding still travelled well within his comfort zone as the field rounded the bend on the approach to three from home where he took off from outside of the wings and touched down with a narrow advantage before being headed and rousted along as the pace notably increased.

Once he hit full stride he was back alongside the eventual winner as they started to draw clear and a further good leap at the penultimate fence helped him keep his momentum. Firmly ridden on the turn for home, the bay dug deep but dropped a few lengths off the leader before taking the last and renewing his effort on the run to the line.

He was never going to catch the winner, who was pushed out under hands and heels riding but it was encouraging to see him battle so gallantly after being up in the van for so long.

I liked what I saw of him at the sale at Aintree in April where he sold to Roger Brookhouse for £170,000. He's a gorgeous-looking gelding with a good deal of bone and scope. He will make a chaser further down the line.

He is the first runner out of his dam who is a full sister to Champion Bumper winner Cheltenian. The further family link back to the useful Prince Taime, who won a bumper before being successful over hurdles, including placed efforts in the Listed Gerry Feilden and the Imperial Cup. He later won over fences.

Big Bresil has all the right credentials to perform to a good level.

BLEUE AWAY
5YR BAY MARE

TRAINER:	Anthony Honeyball
PEDIGREE:	Getaway – Majorite Bleue (Bonbon Rose)
FORM (P2P):	11 -
OPTIMUM TRIP:	2m +
GOING:	Good

This mare looks to have a touch of class.

The strongly made daughter of Getaway made her debut for trainer Philip Rowley in an English point-to-point bumper at Bangor in March where she made all the running under Alex Edwards, pulling away on the run-in to win by a comfortable five lengths from Full Of Roque who has since placed twice, including under Rules at Exeter.

Bleue Away then made it two from two just over a month later in an open 2m4f maiden point-to-point at Eyton-on-Severn, again bounding to the front as the flags went up, jumping well and travelling comfortably before stretching effortlessly clear from the third last to win by an unextended 30 lengths.

The five-year-old comes from a speedy family. Her dam is an unraced half-sister to five winners, including Six Fois Sept (French 1m7f hurdle/2m1f chase) – dam of bumper/hurdle/Flat stayer Pique Sous.

Purchased by Anthony Honeyball at the Tattersalls Cheltenham Sale in May, she could look well bought for £60,000.

Speed is most definitely her forte and she could be hard to peg back in a bumper, or over hurdles if allowed an uncontested lead.

BLOSSOMING FORTH
4YR BAY FILLY

TRAINER:	Ruth Jefferson
PEDIGREE:	Flemensfirth – Blossom Trix (Saddlers' Hall)
FORM (P2P):	1
OPTIMUM TRIP:	2m +
GOING:	Good to Soft

☆ **STAR POTENTIAL** ☆

Blossoming Forth created a new record for a filly or mare from the British point-to-point field when selling for £130,000.

The well-bred daughter of champion sire Flemensfirth won hard held on her debut at Eyton-on-Severn in early May where admittedly she had very little to beat but the manner with which she went about her business was impressive and professional.

Expertly prepared by Philip Rowley and ridden to perfection by top amateur Alex Edwards, the four-year-old travelled well within her comfort zone and readily drew clear once allowed an inch of rein over the final three fences up the home straight. Despite getting a little close to three out and the last, she had so much left in the tank it simply didn't matter as she went on to win without breaking sweat.

The filly is a full sister to useful 2m-3m hurdle/very useful chase winner Beg To Differ and five-year-old Ashtown Lad who has placed twice from three starts in point-to-points. Her dam is an unraced half-sister to bumper/2m-3m hurdle/useful chaser Splendour. The further family link back to smart 2m-2m3f jump winner Atone.

David Minton of Highflyer Bloodstock purchased her as a three-year-old at the Derby Sale in Ireland for €26,000 before selling to Bobby O'Ryan at the Doncaster Sale in May of this year. She will now enter training at Ruth Jefferson's yard who also bought an unraced full sister to Blossoming Forth at the Goffs Land Rover Sale in June for €22,000.

Following the sale of Blossoming Forth, Ruth said, "She's a lovely mare and both of us loved her when we saw her. She'll only improve for a summer off too. There are plenty of mares' races and traditionally we've done well with mares so we're very happy to buy another one. She's been bought for an existing owner in the yard."

Blossoming Forth looks to have plenty of natural ability. She should be capable of winning a bumper but will most definitely come into her own over staying distances, in time.

BOBHOPEORNOHOPE
4YR BAY GELDING

TRAINER:	Kim Bailey
PEDIGREE:	Westerner – Bandelaro (Beneficial)
FORM (P2P):	1 -
OPTIMUM TRIP:	2m 4f +
GOING:	Soft/Heavy

Bobhopeornohope possesses plenty of size to develop into a chaser further down the line.

Trained by Cormac Doyle, the gelding was one of six newcomers when making his debut in the colours of Monbeg Farm Racing Syndicate at Dromahane in mid-April and was partnered by Shane O'Rourke.

Despite his inexperience the four-year-old led or disputed the pace throughout and was still travelling comfortably when he made a slight error at the third from home. He had jumped confidently up until that point, but a further mistake at the next meant he dropped to third place before responding well to regain momentum on the approach to the last. Almost back on an even keel, a final blunder didn't help his cause, but it's a testament to his willing attitude and tenacity that he was not only able to get back up to lead on the line but to win with something in hand.

By Westerner out of a Beneficial mare, he is a half-brother to Mrs Davies who has shown promise for Keith Dalgleish. His dam is an unraced half-sister to the useful 2m-2m4f hurdle/chase winner Marlbrook, 2m-2m4f hurdle winner I'm A Game Changer and 2m3f hurdle winner Indefensible. His further family link back to Grand National winner Corbiere.

Bought at Cheltenham's April Sale by Aiden Murphy and Kim Bailey for £105,000, the gelding will now run in the colours of Mr John Perriss who owns the likes of Rocky's Treasure.

It may take time for Bobhopeornohope to reach his full potential but his attitude and determination will help him in the meantime.

BOLD ASSASSIN
4YR BAY GELDING

TRAINER:	Henry De Bromhead
PEDIGREE:	Golden Lariat – Drumnaskea (Deploy)
FORM (P2P):	2 -
OPTIMUM TRIP:	2m 4f +
GOING:	Soft

Henry De Bromhead has a nice sort to unleash this season.

The Warren Ewing-trained gelding lost nothing in defeat when narrowly denied by the well-regarded Slip Road on his debut in a 2m4f four-year-olds' maiden at Oldtown back in February.

The pace was a steady one from the outset and the field were still tightly grouped as they approached five out where this gelding shaded a narrow advantage. He lost his lead upon touching down to the eventual winner but continued to travel at ease and popped nicely over the next before holding his position as the group climbed to the top of the hill.

Very little separated three runners as they jumped the third from home, but Bold Assassin was caught flat-footed as the pace increased on the downhill section and he had to be cajoled along to maintain his position. A good leap at the penultimate fence kept him well in contention and he responded well to more vigorous driving from Jamie Codd upon touching down.

Not to be denied without a fight, the bay lengthened his stride on the run to the last and threw in a huge leap which saw him touch down in front before running off a true line as the winner found the better turn of foot to pip him by a short head at the post.

This was a hugely admirable performance from Bold Assassin. He showed plenty of potential and it's to his great credit that he was able to lay down such a strong challenge despite losing his pitch as the pace increased. He's a big raw horse and possibly lacked the tactical speed of his competitor.

His sire, Golden Lariat, is a great influence of stamina and has produced strong stayers Dingo Dollar and the ill-fated Fayette County. His dam is an unraced half-sister to a 2m hurdle and chase winner Bravery and 2m5f-3m3f chaser Fornaught Alliance. The further family links back to Foxrock, Death Duty and Beakstown.

Purchased by Henry De Bromhead for £150,000 at the Cheltenham February Sale, it won't be long before he starts repaying his way under Rules.

He could develop into a top-class staying novice hurdler.

BOLD CONDUCT
5YR BAY GELDING

TRAINER:	Colin Tizzard
PEDIGREE:	Stowaway – Vics Miller (Old Vic)
FORM (P2P):	1 -
OPTIMUM TRIP:	2m 4f +
GOING:	Soft

★ **STAR POTENTIAL** ★

A huge son of Stowaway who could develop into a high-class individual.

Bold Conduct towered above his opposition as he made his debut in an above-average four-year-olds' maiden at Loughanmore last November where the pace was ferocious from the outset.

Richie Deegan ensured his mount settled into a good rhythm in the early stages and bided his time in the middle of the pack before progressing through the field as the race developed. Still hard on the steel at five out, the gelding glided into third place at the fourth from home and continued to hold that position before lengthening his stride to take him into second as he produced a decent leap at the penultimate fence.

The tempo increased significantly on the long swing into the home straight as Sidi Ismael attempted to put the race to bed, but Bold Conduct's ground-eating stride enabled him to keep tabs on the leader before jumping to the front over the last and stretching clear up the run-in to win by two and a half lengths with a further 12 back to the third.

This was a properly run race which clocked the fastest time set on the day by some margin. The form also looks strong as the runner-up has since won a bumper by eight lengths for Keith Dalgleish, whilst the fourth won a point and was sold in May to Gerry Hogan for £26,000.

A full brother to Harry Whittington's Speedy Cargo who has placed twice from five starts under Rules. His dam is an unraced half-sister to 2m1f-3m6f hurdle/chase (including cross-country) winner Maljimar, bumper/2m-3m hurdle/useful chaser winner Kymandjen and bumper/useful 2m3f-2m5f hurdle/chase winner Like A Lion.

I had a good look at him as he paraded around the sales ring at Cheltenham in November where he sold to Colin Tizzard for £150,000. He really is a humongous individual, not gangly or ungainly but a powerhouse who will undoubtedly take time to fill his frame. It's a testament to his natural ability that he was able to show so much, never mind win a point-to-point at such an early stage of his development.

Tracks like Newbury, Chepstow and Ascot where he can really use his stride will be ideal.

BRAVEMANSGAME
4YR BAY GELDING

TRAINER:	Paul Nicholls
PEDIGREE:	Brave Mansonnien – Genifique (Nickname)
FORM (P2P):	1 -
OPTIMUM TRIP:	2m 4f +
GOING:	Soft/Heavy

A physically imposing chasing type.

This French-bred gelding became Brave Mansonnien's first runner in an Irish point-to-point when contesting a competitive 11-runner maiden at Lingstown in early March and looks the type who could give his sire a handsome reputation.

Bravemansgame always travelled powerfully up with the pace and did well to survive a bad mistake at the seventh fence which almost had James Walsh on the floor. With momentum restored, the pair regained their position before taking the lead with a good jump at the third from home and quickened impressively with a race-winning move on the downhill run to the next. A spectacular leap there left the race in no doubt as the gelding kept up the relentless gallop to the last before coasting up the run-in to win by an easy eight lengths, recording a time 13 seconds quicker than any other race on the card.

This was a serious performance which impressed Tom Malone and Paul Nicholls who purchased the gelding at the Cheltenham Festival Sale in March for £370,000. He is now owned by Bryan Drew and John Dance.

A first foal, his dam was well beaten over hurdles in France but is a half-sister to the useful 2m2f-3m hurdle/chase winner Sagalyrique and French 2m3f Grade 2 hurdle winner Gray Steel.

Bravemansgame stands at 17 hands tall and will take time to fully develop into his large frame. It's a testament to his natural ability that he was capable of showing so much at an early stage in his career and the future obviously looks bright.

Lingstown is a good test of stamina, which this four-year-old appears to have by the bucketload. He may start off in a bumper, but will probably be seen to best effect over intermediate distances over hurdles and you would fancy him to cope with the midwinter mud given his French pedigree.

BRIEF AMBITION
5YR BAY GELDING

TRAINER:	Fergal O'Brien
PEDIGREE:	Yeats – Kentucky Sky (Cloudings)
FORM (P2P):	321 -
OPTIMUM TRIP:	2m +
GOING:	Good to Soft

☆ **STAR POTENTIAL** ☆

Fergal O'Brien has a smart-looking type on his hands.

Brief Ambition looked for all the winner on his debut at Punchestown's point-to-point track back in February where he quickened into a two-length lead before slamming on the brakes at the final fence. It was a mistake he couldn't recover from but he picked up gamely to snatch third close home. He then finished second at Portrush in March when sent off the odds-on favourite before getting his deserved win at Bellurgan Park two weeks later.

The good-looking gelding travelled well in behind the leaders under Anthony Fox and was still hard on the bridle in third position as he produced a good leap at five from home. He had a long glance at the next but popped over nicely before moving into second place on the quick run to three out. He came up well there and effortlessly went into a share of the lead before extending his advantage with another perfect leap at the penultimate fence.

On the run to the last his jockey stole a look over his shoulder but despite clearly going best of all, he wanted to keep his mount honest and booted him into the fence before sauntering up the run-in to win by a comfortable four lengths.

By Yeats out of a Cloudings mare he has a good pedigree to match his talent. His half-brothers include bumper/2m-2m2f hurdle winner Mystic Sky and 2m-2m4f hurdle winner Iconic Sky. His dam is a bumper winner out of a half-sister to a very smart stayer/useful 2m hurdler Bold Gait and 7f-2m winner/useful 2m hurdler Captain Miller.

Brief Ambition clearly has a decent engine with a turn of foot to boot and will be a force to be reckoned with under Rules for Fergal O'Brien.

He may start off in a bumper but given that he is already five years old, connections may press on over hurdles sooner rather than later.

Brief Ambition – can make an impact for Fergal O'Brien

BROKEN HALO
4YR BAY GELDING

TRAINER:	Paul Nicholls
PEDIGREE:	Kayf Tara – Miss Invincible (Invincible Spirit)
FORM (P2P):	1 -
OPTIMUM TRIP:	2m +
GOING:	Good to Soft

Paul Nicholls has a talented-looking bunch of youngsters at his disposal and this bay gelding is right up there.

The physically imposing son of Kayf Tara was said to be the pick of the paddock when he made his debut for Colin Bowe at Inch in mid-April and was sent off the 9/4 favourite.

Partnered by Barry O'Neill, the pair went to the front for the early part of the contest but were happy to take a lead from Frisson Collonges who pressed on to set a good tempo from the second fence. Still sitting in second spot as the field went over four out, the gelding continued to travel smoothly before being urged to take closer order jumping three from home.

He still appeared full of running as he touched down around half a length adrift of the leader and edged a touch closer before being produced to lead over the penultimate fence. O'Neill kept the gelding up to his work on the run to the last but as he hit the rising ground he found an extra gear before jumping the fence in his stride to draw clear on the climb to the line to win by two and a half lengths.

This was a good performance from the debutant who displayed a very likeable attitude and Tom Malone standing alongside Paul Nicholls was keen to snap him up at the Cheltenham April Sale when parting with £110,000.

A full brother to Gordon Elliott's useful five-time winner John Monash (2m-3m hurdle) and Officer Cadet. His dam placed over 1m2f and is out of a 1m2f-winning half-sister to 6f Group 2 winner Please Sing and Group-placed 7f-1m2f winner Mountain Song.

With plenty of speed in Broken Halo's pedigree, connections may be keen to try him in bumpers before tackling obstacles.

CAPTAIN BLACKPEARL
5YR CHESTNUT GELDING

TRAINER: Tom George
PEDIGREE: Black Sam Bellamy - Bonne Anniversaire (Alflora)
FORM (P2P): 2 -
OPTIMUM TRIP: 2m 4f +
GOING: Soft

★ STAR POTENTIAL ★

Captain Blackpearl made a hugely eye-catching debut to finish second in a hotly contested 17-runner five-year-old geldings' maiden at Dungarvan in late January for Thomas Barry.

The chestnut was held up in arrears for the main part of the contest where he travelled strongly before making stealthy progress through the field on the run to three from home. He jumped the fence in his stride and in the blink of an eye had latched himself on to the leading group before another foot-perfect leap at the penultimate fence allowed him to glide effortlessly around the outside of the tightly bunched field to take up second position.

At that point the leader quickened into a two-length advantage which caught this gelding a little flat-footed, but once finding top stride he began to bridge the deficit on the run to the last, only to have his momentum checked when making a mistake. Despite picking up quickly, he couldn't quite match the turn of foot from Getaway Pat as he scampered away to win by three lengths.

The winner has since entered training with Henry De Bromhead carrying the colours of Philip Reynolds, whilst the third home, Ask A Honey Bee went on to win and is now with Fergal O'Brien. Both feature in this book.

Captain Blackpearl is a full brother to 2m4f hurdle winner Samedi Soir and point winner Bellamy. His half-brothers include hurdle winners Grey Missile (2m5f), Mister Hendre (2m) and Legend Of France (2m). His dam is an unraced sister to the useful 2m hurdler Alph.

This gelding looks a proper old-fashioned galloper and his debut under Rules for Tom George is eagerly awaited.

CARRY ON THE MAGIC
5YR BAY/BROWN GELDING

TRAINER:	Paul Nicholls
PEDIGREE:	Jeremy – Bisoguet (Definite Article)
FORM (P2P):	2 -
OPTIMUM TRIP:	2m +
GOING:	Soft

Carry On The Magic will be easy to spot on the track with his big white blaze.

The good-looking son of Jeremy looks to possess plenty of size and has been given time to mature by Paul Nicholls following his narrow defeat by the well-regarded Killer Clown on his debut at Corbeagh House in early December.

He always travelled smoothly on the soft ground and steadily moved into contention down the far side before a good leap at the fourth from home gave him momentum which he carried to the lead before the next. Appearing to be going best of all, he managed to pull two lengths clear on the uphill section and found an extra gear on the bend before the final two fences.

Looking the likely winner, the gelding had a couple of lengths in hand as he produced a spring-heeled leap over the penultimate fence and responded well to Jimmy O'Rourke on the run to the last where he came up well when asked to find a stride. Despite doing his best, he appeared to tire on the run to the line and the winner managed to win by a length, with a further 10 back to the third.

Carry On The Magic is the first foal out of the French-trained mare Bisoguet who placed over hurdles and fences up to 2m4f. She is a sister to 2m4f/2m6f chase winner Doctor Pat and a half-sister to useful 2m-2m4f hurdle/chase winner The West's Awake out of 1m4f Flat/high-class 2m-2m3f jump winner, Makounji.

Purchased by Tom Malone and Paul Nicholls at the December Sale for £160,000, this gelding looks to have a bright future and will carry the colours of Highclere Thoroughbred Racing.

Carry On The Magic has a tremendous physique and covers plenty of ground with his long-reaching stride. He should have no problem getting off the mark over hurdles, although soft ground may see him in the best light.

CILL ANNA
4YR BAY FILLY

TRAINER:	Paul Nicholls
PEDIGREE:	Imperial Monarch – Technohead (Distinctly North)
FORM (P2P):	1 -
OPTIMUM TRIP:	2m
GOING:	Good to Soft

Set to carry the colours of Andy Stewart. Cill Anna is surely one to note on the bumper scene this season.

This bonny-looking daughter of Imperial Monarch made her debut in a hotly contested 13-runner maiden at Monksgrange at the end of March where Barry O'Neill elected to keep things simple.

Sent to the front shortly after the flags went up, the filly set an honest gallop but momentarily lost her lead when outjumped at the fifth from home before regaining her position on the run to the next. Again, she wasn't foot perfect, but continued to travel strongly and was better at the next before pulling a length clear on the uphill turn into the home straight.

The pace notably increased when she was joined on the run down to the penultimate fence but the filly kept finding for pressure and popped over neatly before battling gamely on the sprint to the last. Despite a slightly fiddly leap, she quickly found her stride and was not for passing as she clung on courageously to win by a head from Who's The Boss.

By Imperial Monarch out of a Distinctly North mare, she's not bred to be a three-mile chaser, but more of a speedster over much shorter trips. She is a half-sister to bumper/2m-2m3f hurdle/chase winner Distime, bumper/2m hurdle winner Half The Odds and point winner Summoned. Her dam was a 2m3f hurdle winner who is a half-sister to a 1m4f Group 3 winner.

Tom Malone and Paul Nicholls were responsible for signing the docket for £115,000 at the Grand National Sale in April and bumpers will probably now await for this tremendously game individual.

CLONDAW CAITLIN
4YR BAY FILLY

TRAINER:	Ruth Jefferson
PEDIGREE:	Court Cave – Kilmessan (Flemensfirth)
FORM (P2P):	P - F2
OPTIMUM TRIP:	2m 4f +
GOING:	Good

Clondaw Caitlin showed plenty of promise on her most recent start for Michael Goff and is open to plenty of improvement for her new connections.

The good-looking daughter of Court Cave returned home sick after pulling up before the penultimate fence on her debut at Ballycahane in a race won by the record-breaking sales purchase My Whirlwind. She then fell at an early stage on her next start at Necarne in mid-May before giving us a glimpse of her ability two days later at Bartlemy to fill out second place under Shane Fitzgerald.

Clondaw Caitlin travelled smoothly in a prominent position throughout the three-mile contest and glided into a share of the lead on the long run to the third from home where she was outjumped by Fantasia Roque. Ridden to reassert her position around the turn for home to face the final two fences, the filly responded generously and pinged the penultimate fence before swooping to the front on the run to the last. Steadied into the fence by her jockey, she lost her momentum and was overtaken in the air by the eventual winner and couldn't quite get back on top, despite doing her best efforts to rally on the run to the line, eventually losing out by half a length.

Victory was decided by the leap at the last, and although this filly lost out, she certainly showed she has plenty of ability to transfer to track success for Ruth Jefferson, who alongside Bobby O'Ryan secured her for a modest sum of £40,000 at the Goffs UK Spring Sale at Doncaster in May.

She is a full sister to Deborah Faulkner's 2m5f hurdle winner Courtinthemiddle and Keith Dalgleish's Tetraites Style. Her dam is an unraced sister to 2m7f-3m hurdle/chase winner Cheat The Cheater and a half-sister to bumper/2m3f-3m1f hurdle/smart chaser winner Takagi and 2m4f-3m hurdle/chase winner Victrix Gale.

Being by Court Cave, I would expect Clondaw Caitlin to appreciate better ground. She also has the stamina in her pedigree to stay a trip in time.

DEFUTURE IS BRIGHT
5YR BAY GELDING

TRAINER:	Christian Williams
PEDIGREE:	Westerner – Dustys Delight (Oscar)
FORM (P2P):	24 - 2
OPTIMUM TRIP:	2m 4f +
GOING:	Good

Defuture Is Bright could be the type to flourish for his new yard.

The strongly made son of Westerner created a lasting impression on his debut at Moig South in November when fighting valiantly all the way to the line, only to be denied by the equally brave Picanha who held on to win by a neck. His enthusiastic way of travelling teamed with his pinpoint accurate jumping was a sight to behold.

The gelding then sold for £135,000 to Noel Meade and Margaret O'Toole at the Cheltenham November Sale before returning to the pointing field in spring. He was beaten into fourth at short odds on his first revisit to the track at Inch but then fared better 11 days later at Dromahane when showing plenty of zest on the front end, only to be denied on the run to the line by the well-regarded The Bull McCabe who now resides at Kim Bailey's yard.

Put back through the ring at the Goffs Doncaster Horses-In-Training Sale in May, he now finds himself in the care of Christian Williams who secured him in a private sale for £50,000.

A half-brother to Katy Price's 2m5f/3m chase winner Out For Justice. His dam is an unraced sister to the smart 2m7f-4m chase winner Tricky Trickster.

Defuture Is Bright looked an above-average individual at the back end of last year, but slightly lost his way before returning to something like his former self on his last start. He may be the type to require time, but there will certainly be races to be won with him – possibly on good ground when tackling a trip. He could equally be hard to peg back if enjoying an uncontested lead over an intermediate distance.

DEPLOY THE GETAWAY
4YR BAY GELDING

TRAINER:	Willie Mullins
PEDIGREE:	Getaway – Gaelic River (Deploy)
FORM (P2P):	1 -
OPTIMUM TRIP:	2m +
GOING:	Soft

★ **STAR POTENTIAL** ★

Deploy The Getaway left a lasting impression on his debut and looks one of the most talented prospects to come from the pointing field this season.

The physically imposing son of Getaway started his career in a four-year-olds' maiden at Tallow in February for Donnchadh Doyle and James Walsh where he was simply in a different stratosphere to his opposition. Booted to the front as the flags went up, the bay was relentless on the front end, jumping with foot-perfect precision and gaining ground at each fence. He still only appeared to be travelling in second gear as he jumped four out with ears pricked and a five-length lead quickly doubled after he sailed over the third from home. By the time he had reached the next, the race was in safekeeping and a mistake at the last did very little to interrupt his momentum as he coasted home to a heavily eased 20-length success.

This really was a head-turning performance and there was no surprise to see him fetch plenty of interest at the Cheltenham Sale in February. Tom Malone and Tessa Greatrex all wanted a piece of the action, but it was Harold Kirk who had the final say when signing the docket to a sum of £200,000. The gelding will now run in the colours of Cheveley Park Stud for trainer Willie Mullins.

The gelding has an impressive pedigree to match his performance. His dam is an unraced half-sister to 3m/3m6f chase winner Bally Braes out of an unraced half-sister to bumper/2m6f-3m3f hurdle/chase winner Special Account and useful 2m4f-3m1f chase winner River Mandalay. From the family of Special Tiara.

Deploy The Getaway obviously has a huge engine and a high cruising speed. His round knee action may lend itself to soft underfoot conditions, but this is a high-class individual and I expect him to be making his way through the ranks to Graded company over the coming seasons.

DIRECT FIRE
4YR BAY GELDING

TRAINER:	Noel Meade
PEDIGREE:	Yeats – Emmylou Du Berlais (Kadalko)
FORM (P2P):	41 -
OPTIMUM TRIP:	2m +
GOING:	Soft

Direct Fire became trainer Brian Hamilton's first winner in the Gigginstown House Stud colours.

The well-related son of Yeats showed good promise to finish fourth on his debut in a competitive maiden at Borris House which was run in abysmal conditions in early March.

He returned on better ground a month later at Moira where Declan Lavery kept things simple, racing in a handy position before nosing to the front on the approach to four out. He continued to vie for the lead on the run to the next where he stood off from outside the wings and landed with a length advantage over the fellow Gigginstown-owned Battle Of Actium which doubled to two lengths as he quickened on the level.

He was still on the bridle as the field climbed the hill towards two from home but he faced a strong challenge from Berties Girl who quickened on the approach and overtook him in the air. Rising to the test, Direct Fire found an extra gear and the pair went toe-to-toe on the downhill run to the last but the better leap from this gelding ensured he got away from the fence quickly and won fairly readily in the end.

Bought for €65,000 as a three-year-old at the Land Rover Sale last summer by Noel Meade. He is a half-brother to bumper/2m-2m1f hurdle/very smart chase winner Mr Mole whose victories included the Grade 2 Game Spirit Chase. He is also a half-brother to 2m2f hurdle winner Wendy Du Berlais, Listed-placed Wallace Du Berlais and 2m1f chase winner Walter Du Berlais.

This looks an athletic model with plenty of speed at his disposal. Bumpers will probably be a good starting point before progressing to obstacles next season.

DO THE FLOSS
4YR BAY GELDING

TRAINER:	Mary E Doyle
PEDIGREE:	Shantou – Hannah Rose (Un Desperado)
FORM (P2P):	4
OPTIMUM TRIP:	2m +
GOING:	Good to Soft

The Baltimore Stables produce top-class point-to-point horses and Do The Floss, although only fourth on his debut, could be one to watch once he is sold.

The four-year-old made his debut under Jonjo O'Neill in a good maiden at Dawstown in early May where he was one of five newcomers in the 10-runner contest and sent off at odds of 8/1.

He travelled smoothly in amongst horses for the majority of the contest but jumping errors started to creep in late on and a bad blunder at the seventh appeared to knock his confidence before a further error at three out completely stopped him in his tracks.

Given time to recover, he steadily regathered his momentum and was helped to see a stride over the penultimate fence before coming up well over the last and staying on nicely up the straight to take fourth position, 18 lengths behind the winner.

Although well beaten there were definite signs of ability and the way he kept plugging on despite his errors was very encouraging. James Doyle told me the gelding had been working well prior to his run and maybe the type to flourish with another season in the pointing field.

His full brother, Zero Ten, was not dissimilar but is obviously thriving now, with a win at Punchestown followed by a victory at the Galway Festival on his chasing debut.

He is also a half-brother to Michael Scudamore's 3m2f chase winner Oriental Fixer. His dam was placed in bumpers and is a half-sister to 2m hurdle winner Dahra One.

Do The Floss is well capable of winning his next point start before being sold either privately or at one of the major sales. Given his pedigree, he will attract plenty of attention.

DOES HE KNOW
4YR BAY GELDING

TRAINER:	Kim Bailey
PEDIGREE:	Alkaased – Diavoleria (Slip Anchor)
FORM (P2P):	1 -
OPTIMUM TRIP:	2m +
GOING:	Good

An interestingly bred gelding by Japan Cup winner Alkaased.

Does He know made his debut under John Dawson at Charm Park in early April for North Yorkshire handler Cherry Coward and became her first debutant four-year-old winner.

The scopey gelding travelled well in behind the leaders and produced a good leap over the open ditch, five from home, before moving into closer contention over the next. He continued his forward progression on the run to three out and jumped into second place before being asked to pick up the leader going into the wings of the penultimate fence.

Challenged on either side as the field took the bend for home, Does He Know had to battle bravely on the run down to the last, but produced a much-needed good leap which helped him quicken away up the run-in to win by a diminishing neck from the fast-finishing runner-up Teescomponents Boy who went on to win next time.

Does He Know is the second foal out of Diavoleria who was trained by Cherry's Dad, Mick Easterby, to win a bumper before being successful over hurdles (2m3f-2m6f) and later fences (3m1f).

There was plenty to like about this performance and Kim Bailey, who paid £38,000 at Cheltenham's April Sale could have a good purchase on his hands.

He has a chaser's physique but clearly showed not to be devoid of a turn of foot and looks an interesting prospect for the novice hurdle division.

ECLAIR ON LINE
5YR BAY GELDING

TRAINER:	Charlie Longsdon
PEDIGREE:	Dream Well – Odeline (Rochesson)
FORM (P2P):	71 -
OPTIMUM TRIP:	2m +
GOING:	Soft

This gelding could look very well bought.

Eclair On Line was given a gentle introduction to racing at Portrush at the end of March when staying on steadily from the rear to finish seventh of 13.

Benefiting from that experience, the French-bred reappeared two weeks later at Loughbrickland where he travelled smoothly and displayed a very willing attitude on the uphill run to three from home before quickening clear under hands and heels riding after landing in front over the penultimate fence. He had opened up a healthy advantage by the time he had reached the last, and a foot-perfect leap there allowed him to come home the impressive eight-length winner.

This was a much-improved performance from his debut, possibly appreciating the greater test of stamina on the soft ground. The form has also appeared strong with both the runner-up and the fifth going on to win their next starts. The favourite Jeremy Sunshine, who pulled up before the last, also went on to win and is now in training with Colin Tizzard having been sold for £30,000.

The gelding comes from a progressive young family. His half-brother Dino Boy won a 2m4f point and was placed second in a bumper at Aintree in May behind the well-regarded Garry Clermont and has subsequently been purchased by Highflyer for £50,000. His other half-brother Foudre Delta placed second in a valuable 2m2f hurdle at Compiegne earlier this year and was sold for €100,000 at Arqana in May. His dam is a twice-raced half-sister to French/Italian 1m7f/2m-3m hurdle/chase winner Kel Ecossaise.

Bought for what could be a steal of a price at £34,000 by Highflyer Bloodstock and Charlie Longsdon at Cheltenham in April. There should be plenty of fun to be had with this progressive-looking sort.

ECLAIR SURF
5YR BAY GELDING

TRAINER:	Emma Lavelle
PEDIGREE:	Califet – Matasurf (Rochesson)
FORM (P2P):	31 -
OPTIMUM TRIP:	2m +
GOING:	Soft/Heavy

The French-bred son of Califet showed good promise despite lacking fluency over his fences on his debut at Lisronagh back in November, but had clearly learnt plenty for that experience when annihilating his opposition at Bandon in March earlier this year.

The imposing gelding bounced out to make all under Jack Hendrick, jumping well throughout and setting an unrelenting gallop which his opposition simply couldn't cope with. More than 10 lengths separated himself from the rest as he splashed his way through the puddles on the downhill run to the last, drawing further clear before popping over the fence and coasting to a very easy 30-length success.

The form may be a little suspect due to the extreme heavy conditions which wouldn't have suited all of his rivals, but the fourth home has since won on good ground and is now in the care of Tim Vaughan. Highway Prince and Scullys Forge, who were both pulled up, have also gone on to win.

Eclair Surf is the second foal out of Matasurf, a French-placed mare over 2m1f-2m5f hurdle/chase (including cross-country). She is a half-sister to 10.5f Flat/2m1f-2m7f hurdle/cross-country chase winner The Surf out of an 11.5f and 1m4f winner.

Purchased as a three-year-old for €44,000 by Monbeg Stables, they got a good return on their investment when Gerry Hogan went to £140,000 to take him home from the Cheltenham Festival Sale in March.

This gelding has a natural blend of speed and stamina and should come into his own when the mud is flying.

EMTARA
4YR BAY FILLY

TRAINER:	Donald McCain
PEDIGREE:	Kayf Tara – Miss Ballantyne (Definite Article)
FORM (P2P):	1 -
OPTIMUM TRIP:	2m 4f +
GOING:	Soft

This well-related daughter of top sire Kayf Tara displayed a very willing attitude to repel all challengers on her debut at Inch in April.

The Colin Bowe-trained four-year-old raced prominently throughout the three-mile contest and still galloped on strongly as the field headed towards the third from home. With ears pricked she came up nicely for Barry O'Neill who pushed her along momentarily upon touching down before she stretched her lead further on the quick approach to two out. Again she jumped with precision but was challenged on the outside by Tune The Chello. Not to be denied, Emtara raised her game and found an extra gear running to the last where she came up out of Barry's hands before fending off her rival on the steep climb to the line to win by two lengths with a further six back to Fantasia Roque.

This was a professional performance by the newcomer and the form has been subsequently boosted by the third home who went on to win next time and has since joined Noel Meade for £70,000. The runner-up was also sold and is now with Henry De Bromhead.

Emtara passed through the sales but was bought back by Colin Bowe for €70,000 at Punchestown in May. She has since been purchased privately by Donald McCain and will race in the colours of Tim Leslie.

Emtara is the first produce of Miss Ballantyne who was trained by Nicky Henderson to win a 2m4f novice hurdle and a 3m handicap chase. She is a full sister to 3m hurdle winner Dundee and a half-sister to 2m5f-4m chase winner and Grand National sixth-placed Royale Knight, very useful 2m-3m hurdle/chase winner Frisco Depot and useful 2m-3m2f chase winner Cool Operator.

This filly looks sure to have a smart career on the track.

ESCARIA TEN
5YR BAY GELDING

TRAINER:	Gordon Elliott
PEDIGREE:	Maresca Sorrento – Spartes Eria (Ballingarry)
FORM (P2P):	1 -
OPTIMUM TRIP:	2m 4f +
GOING:	Soft

★ **STAR POTENTIAL** ★

Escaria Ten is a potentially high-class individual to join Gordon Elliott's stable.

The extremely athletic son of Maresca Sorrento was well touted before the off on his debut at Borris House in March for trainer Liam Lennon and was sent off at odds of 4/6 under Jamie Codd.

Conditions were atrocious for the three-mile contest and the ground was officially described as soft, but this gelding showed no signs of unease as he tracked the leaders in what appeared to be no more than a hack canter. He also looked extremely accomplished in the jumping department and a foot-perfect leap allowed him to touch down in second position over the fourth from home. Still travelling well within himself on the run to the next, he was again pinpoint accurate and moved into a narrow advantage before extending his lead on the downhill run to the penultimate fence.

With ears pricked, he sailed over the fence and quickened on the short run to the last where a final spectacular leap allowed him to comfortably extend his lead to two and a half lengths at the line from Lifeisahighway, with a further 15-length break back to the third.

Purchased as a three-year-old by Peter Molony of Rathmore Stud for £45,000 he has since joined Cullentra House Stables in a private deal.

A first foal, his dam is an unraced half-sister to French 2m1f/2m2f hurdle winner Rex Quercus, out of French Listed-placed 1m/10/f winner Kassaboum. From the further family of Grade 3 chase winner Subehargues and Belle Yepa (dam of the high-class Whisper).

Given his scope and age, he may go straight over hurdles, but wherever he begins his career under Rules, I fully expect him to make an huge impact.

EVANDER
4YR BROWN GELDING

TRAINER:	Oliver Greenall
PEDIGREE:	Arcadio – Blazing Belle (Presenting)
FORM (P2P):	1 -
OPTIMUM TRIP:	2m +
GOING:	Good to Soft

Evander looks a nice prospect for a lower profile yard.

The son of Arcadio made his debut in April at Taylorstown and sat in fourth position going out on to the final circuit but slightly lost his pitch as the pace increased over the fourth from home. Rob James appeared happy enough aboard the gelding and bided his time before making a move into the wings of three out where a good leap enabled him to recover some ground and move into third position.

He continued his forward move on the steep downhill run towards the penultimate fence and breezed into second place before producing a good leap on the incline. Ridden along on the tight bend towards the last, the gelding responded generously for pressure and joined the leader in the air before fighting bravely on the run to the line to repel Battle Of Actium by one and a half lengths.

The form has subsequently worked out very well. The runner-up went on to beat the fourth next time whilst The Whiskey Man, who was beaten out of sight in seventh, went on to be a close third next time and Largy Fix, who fell at the penultimate fence, won by four lengths on his next start.

Oliver Greenall purchased this gelding for a modest £30,000 at Doncaster in May to run in the colours of Highclere Thoroughbred Racing. He also bought the third home, Clondaw Pretender for £27,000.

Evander is the second foal out of Blazing Belle who is an unraced daughter of 2m4f bumper/hurdle winner Blazing Missile. Herself a half-sister to bumper/Listed 2m2f hurdle winner Blazing Sky and useful 2m3f-2m6f hurdle/chase winner Blazing Beacon.

This looks a tough gelding with plenty of speed to match his stamina. He could be a little bit of value when making his debut.

EXOD'ELA
5YR BAY GELDING

TRAINER:	Jamie Snowden
PEDIGREE:	Saddler Maker – Queen'ela (Robin Des Champs)
FORM (P2P):	1 -
OPTIMUM TRIP:	2m +
GOING:	Soft

Exod'ela received a very good ride to come from last to first to make a winning debut and could be an above average sort.

The athletic son of Saddler Maker was one of four newcomers when embarking on his career between the flags in a five and six-year olds' maiden at Lismore in early March where he was put to sleep at the rear of the field by Derek O'Connor. The strong-travelling type still had most of the field in front of him going over the fourth from home and appeared in no hurry as he popped over the next before making steady headway into sixth position at the penultimate fence.

Asked to improve on the run to the last, the gelding picked up impressively and quickened into contention in a matter of strides, almost jumping the fence alongside the leader until landing awkwardly, causing him to lose momentum. After quickly regathering his stride, the bay motored around the bend for home and picked up the lead on the run-in to win by a cosy two and a half lengths from Three Is Company who was benefiting from experience.

Purchased as a three-year-old in June 2017 at the Goffs Land Rover Store Sale for €43,000, he then went unsold for £24,000 later that year before being picked up for £80,000 by Tom Malone and Jamie Snowden at the Cheltenham Festival Sale in March.

A half-brother to French winners Amour'Ela (1m4f-2m AQPS Flat) and Codd'Ela (2m1f chase). His dam placed over 1m4f-1m6f AQPS Flat and is granddaughter to a 2m5f cross-country chase winner.

Exod'ela isn't the biggest but he appears to have a natural blend of speed and stamina. He also looked at home in the testing conditions and will most likely start over hurdles.

Derek O'Connor – cool, calm and collected

FADO DES BROSSES
4YR BAY GELDING

TRAINER:	Evan Williams
PEDIGREE:	Balko – Nanou Des Brosses (Saint Cyrien)
FORM (P2P):	1 -
OPTIMUM TRIP:	2m 4f +
GOING:	Soft

This son of Balko looks blessed with a useful turn of foot and could be an above-average prospect for Evan Williams to go to town with this season.

Fado Des Brosses made his debut for Pat Doyle in a four-year-olds' maiden at Belharbour in early February, a race the trainer has a good record in having previously trained the likes of Dorrells Pierji to success two years ago.

The French-bred gelding was given a patient ride on his racecourse introduction from Johnny Barry who held him up in arrears before making progress going out on to the final circuit. Still travelling with confidence, the gelding recovered well from a bad mistake at four out to make significant progress on the uphill rise to three from home where he produced a super leap, landing with momentum before quickening impressively on the turn into the straight.

Almost alongside the two leaders at the penultimate fence, he got in a little close but continued to motor to the last and had just poked his nose to the front when Goaheadwiththeplan took a tumble leaving him to come home an easy 15-length winner. Even without his departure, Fado Des Brosses appeared to have his measure and crossed the line in the manner of a horse with plenty more to give.

The form has yet to be fully tested, but that didn't stop Evan Williams paying £200,000 to take the gelding home from the Cheltenham Sale in February. He will now run in the colours of Mr & Mrs William Rucker.

A half-brother to the useful 2m3f-2m7f hurdle winner Cobolobo. His dam is a 1m4f AQPS Flat winner and is a sister to French 2m3f/2m4f hurdle winner Lutin Des Brosses, and half-sister to 2m1f-2m6f (including Listed) chase winner Sarah Des Brosses.

Judging by the gelding's success, he has plenty of speed and a potent turn of foot but should also stay a trip when needed. He won on a good to yielding surface, but he has a ground-grabbing action which lends itself to softer conditions.

FAROUK D'ALENE
4YR BAY GELDING

TRAINER:	Gordon Elliott
PEDIGREE:	Racinger – Mascotte D'Alene (Ragmar)
FORM (P2P):	1 -
OPTIMUM TRIP:	2m +
GOING:	Soft

★ **STAR POTENTIAL** ★

Gordon Elliott looks to have a talented one on his hands here.

Farouk D'Alene made his debut in what looked on paper to be a competitive little five-runner four-year-olds' maiden at Belclare in March – a race previously won by Best Mate, and more recently Topofthegame for these same connections.

The Donnchadh Doyle-trained gelding travelled strongly in a share of the lead before gaining a length as he touched down on the landing side of five out. He continued to force his advantage over the next where he was ridden to see a stride before pressing on as he went through the gears to jump three out with a commanding lead.

Jimmy O'Rourke stole a glance over his right shoulder on the turn-in where he was five lengths clear before the gelding took the penultimate fence in his stride and continued to open up his advantage by the best part of 12 lengths before the last. A slight mistake there did little to interrupt his momentum as he coasted home to win by an easy 18 lengths with a further 15 back to the only other finisher.

This was a visually impressive performance backed up by the clock which recorded a time 13 seconds faster than average.

As a three-year-old he fetched £34,000 at the Doncaster Store Sale in

May 2018 but connections received a hefty return for their money when Margaret O'Toole acting on behalf of Gordon Elliott went to £260,000 at the Cheltenham Festival Sale in March.

There is very little to speak of in his immediate pedigree, but the likes of Triolo D'Alene and Arpege D'Alene feature further down the page. It's easy to get carried away when a horse produces a performance like the one which Farouk D'Alene did and he has gone to the right stable to make his presence felt under Rules.

To the eye, he looks to be quite an easy-going sort who will probably get a trip, although his turn of foot may see him competitive earlier in his career if tackling bumpers.

FERNY HOLLOW
4YR BAY/BROWN GELDING

TRAINER:	Willie Mullins
PEDIGREE:	Westerner – Mirazur (Good Thyne)
FORM (P2P):	1 -
OPTIMUM TRIP:	2m 4f +
GOING:	Soft

★ **STAR POTENTIAL** ★

A very exciting addition to Willie Mullins' team.

There was plenty to like about the performance of the Colin Bowe-trained four-year-old as he romped his way to success in a 2m4f maiden against his own age group at Knockanard back in February.

The son of Westerner was taken to the front by Jimmy O'Rourke where he travelled comfortably whilst setting a brisk tempo. He was still leading the march at the fourth from home, but he got in far too close and was shuffled back into third position before salvaging momentum and reasserting himself at the head of the pack.

On the downhill run to the next, he upped the ante and jumped the fence in his stride but was far from tidy at the second from home which is taken on the uphill rise before the bend into the straight. That error could've been enough to knock the stuffing out of him, but he marched on with purpose and pulled a few lengths clear of his nearest pursuer before popping over the last to draw right away to win by an eased-down 15 lengths.

This race was won last year by Colin Bowe's hugely exciting prospect Shadow Rider, who is yet to emerge, and this gelding looks cut from the same cloth. He should make a big impact under Rules for his new trainer, Willie Mullins, who alongside Harold Kirk went to £300,000 to take him home from the Cheltenham Festival Sale.

The form doesn't look anything special and the only one to give it a little boost was Bloodstone who finished second and went on to fill out the same position on his next start. Nevertheless, the manner with which this gelding crossed the line suggested he won with any amount in hand and was simply in a different parish to the rest.

This is a family Mullins knows well having trained the gelding's half-sisters Vittorio and the useful Chiltern Hills, whilst his dam is an unraced half-sister to the useful jumper Hersov.

Set to carry the colours of Cheveley Park Stud, it's anyone's guess how much ability the gelding has, but the potential is there for all to see.

I would expect him to be most effective when there is a little give underfoot over an intermediate trip, but I fully expect him to make an impact in bumpers before switching codes.

Cheveley Park Stud – so successful with Envoi Allen and Malone Road (pictured)

FILOU DES ISSARDS
4YR CHESTNUT GELDING

TRAINER: Philip Hobbs
PEDIGREE: Network – Rapiere (Video Rock)
FORM (P2P): 3 -
OPTIMUM TRIP: 2m +
GOING: Soft

There should be plenty more to come from this fellow.

Filou Des Issards caught the eye when filling out third position on his debut at Dawstown in May where he made a couple of fiddly errors over the final two fences before staying on kindly behind Face The Odds and Totally Rejected, who have since sold to Noel Meade and Donald McCain respectively – the former for £165,000.

In the colours of Tim Hyde, the son of Network travelled well throughout the three-mile contest, if not a little green at times, but made good progress to move into fourth position at the third from home. Kept up to his work, the gelding stayed on willingly on the uphill run to take third position before the penultimate fence, where despite making a mistake, he picked up courageously and continued at the one pace towards the final fence before being pushed out to secure his position, 13 lengths behind the winner.

He's not an obvious inclusion in this book but he has plenty of scope and given his distinct signs of inexperience teamed with the possibility that he may enjoy softer conditions, there is a strong case to suggest there is plenty more to come. He could look well bought by Philip Hobbs, who parted with £42,000 at the Goffs UK Spring Sale in May.

His pedigree screams stamina given that he is by Network out of a Video Rock mare, but he is a half-brother to Clemsy, a 1m3f/1m4f AQPS Flat winner. His dam is a 1m2f-1m4f AQPS winner and is a half-sister to multiple Flat winners Ouragan Du Bouchat (1m4f), 2m1f hurdle/2m6f chase winner Kaolin James and 2m4f Chase winner Namous.

Filou Des Issards may not be a world-beater but he looks more than capable of track success for his new connections.

GABBYS CROSS
4YR BAY GELDING

TRAINER:	Henry De Bromhead
PEDIGREE:	Frammassone - Mille Et Un Nuits (Ecologist)
FORM (P2P):	1
OPTIMUM TRIP:	2m 4f +
GOING:	Good to Soft

Roger Brookhouse has bought a number of quality-looking point-to-pointers this season and this son of Frammassone is right up there.

Gabbys Cross was never too far off the pace as he embarked on his debut at Monksgrange in late April and was still well within his comfort zone as he popped over five from home where he went into third position. He continued to make progress into second over the next before applying further pressure to the leader on the uphill climb after taking three from home.

On the bend into the straight the gelding showed a good turn of foot in response to Tom Hamilton's urgings which caught his opposition on the hop as the pair extended into a two-length lead approaching the penultimate fence. They got over well and continued to grind away in front before a final good leap at the last allowed him to extend his lead to four lengths at the line from Frisco Bay who was benefiting from experience.

Gabbys Cross looks a real galloping sort with a liking for soft ground. He is a half-brother to the Sam Thomas-trained 2m4f-2m5f chase winner Not A Role Model. His dam achieved very little in bumpers but is a half-sister to nine jump winners, including the smart 2m-2m5f hurdle/useful 2m4f chase winner Mister Banjo.

Purchased for €170,000 at the Punchestown Sale in May by Roger Brookhouse. The gelding is likely to start paying his way when the emphasis is on stamina.

GENERATION TEXT
4YR BAY GELDING

TRAINER:	Dan Skelton
PEDIGREE:	Getaway – Maid In Glenavy (King's Theatre)
FORM (P2P):	2 -
OPTIMUM TRIP:	2m 4f +
GOING:	Soft

Dan Skelton acquired Generation Text to run in the colours of Highclere Thoroughbred Racing.

The strongly made son of Getaway created a good impression on his debut at Borris House when finishing second behind Sporting John in a hotly contested four-year-old maiden. The gelding travelled supremely well throughout the three-mile contest and moved stylishly into contention after the third from home. On the approach to the penultimate fence he displayed a notable turn of foot which carried him to the front on the quick run to the last but a slight mistake there cost him valuable momentum and the eventual winner breezed on by to a two-and-a-half length victory.

The form has a very strong look to it as the winner, Sporting John, has since fetched £160,000 and will carry the colours of J P McManus, whilst the third, fourth and fifth have all won on their next starts.

By Getaway out of a King's Theatre mare, his dam is an unraced daughter to Noel Meade's 1m Flat/very useful 2m hurdle winner Miss Emer.

Generation Text is a powerfully built gelding who covers plenty of ground. He should be ready to make an impact this season and then progress with a step up in trip further down the line.

GERALDO
4YR BAY GELDING

TRAINER:	Gordon Elliott
PEDIGREE:	Jeremy – Jim's Article (Definite Article)
FORM (P2P):	1
OPTIMUM TRIP:	2m +
GOING:	Good

Geraldo looks to have a touch of class.

The son of Jeremy was put to sleep towards the rear of the 10-runner field on his debut in a four-year-olds' maiden at Stowlin before being produced to lead on the line under a wonderfully well-timed ride by Derek O'Connor.

The gelding always travelled well within himself off the pace on the first circuit before making noticeable headway into sixth position at the fifth from home. He continued his forward move over the next and quickened into closer contention on the bend before the penultimate fence, which he jumped well. He still had around four lengths to find on the leaders at the last, but upon touching down his jockey asked for maximum effort and the gelding responded generously to find an extra gear, staying on strongly to win with something in hand from Don Diablo.

Bloodstock agent Aidan O'Ryan acting on behalf of Gordon Elliott purchased Geraldo at the Goffs Doncaster Sale in August for £66,000. He also bought the runner-up earlier in the year for £70,000.

Geraldo is the first foal out of Jim's Article, an unraced sister to the Howard Johnson-trained bumper/2m hurdle winner Striking Article, David Pipe-trained bumper/2m hurdle winner Raichu and the Katy Price 2m4f hurdle winner Definite Winner.

This speedy sort is likely to pave his way in bumpers this season.

get on it now I see it

GETAWAY PAT
5YR CHESTNUT GELDING

TRAINER:	Henry De Bromhead
PEDIGREE:	Getaway – Sunset Gold (Supreme Leader)
FORM (P2P):	1 -
OPTIMUM TRIP:	2m 4f +
GOING:	Soft

★ **STAR POTENTIAL** ★

Getaway Pat could be Philip Reynolds' next future star. *Future Chaser*

Pat Doyle's debutant looked a complete natural on the track when he made his debut at Dungarvan in a five-year-olds' maiden in late January and now enters training with Henry De Bromhead.

The gelding travelled effortlessly on the pace and held a narrow advantage at the third from home where he never broke stride and maintained his position at the front. He continued to bound along with ears pricked over the next before opening up his advantage once given an inch of rein on the turn for home.

He quickly shot a few lengths clear after being given a squeeze from John Barry in the saddle and produced a foot-perfect leap at the last to send him charging up the run-in to win by three lengths from Tom Barry's hugely eye-catching Captain Blackpearl, with a further 10-length break back to Ask A Honey Bee.

This was a hugely exciting debut from the son of Getaway. The manner with which he quickened and powered away from the back of the last was indicative of a performer who had plenty more to give.

Connections were keen to bide their time and wait for some ease in the ground before allowing him to run. He's a big, strong and imposing sort and I think going forward soft ground will be important to him as he has a very round knee action. He was entered at the Punchestown Festival earlier in the season but didn't run, possibly on account of the ground being too quick.

His dam is an unraced sister to bumper/2m4f hurdle/chase winner Deep Sunset, half-sister to bumper/2m5f-3m2f hurdle winner Glacial Sunset and useful 2m3f/2m5f hurdle winner Bobbina.

As the cliché goes, whatever he achieves this season will be a bonus. He's a chaser for the future with the potential to reach the very top.

GIANTS TABLE
4YR BROWN GELDING

TRAINER:	Nicky Henderson
PEDIGREE:	Great Pretender – Bold Fire (Bold Edge)
FORM (P2P):	1 -
OPTIMUM TRIP:	2m 4f+
GOING:	Soft

This gelding looks a proper stayer in the making.

The Colin Bowe-trained Giants Table was one of nine newcomers when making his debut in atrocious weather conditions at Ballycahane's County Limerick track in early March under Barry O'Neill and was said to fill the eye in the paddock.

The four-year-old looked a strong travelling sort and continually caught the eye as he moved with ease behind the leaders before the fourth from home. He continued to bide his time in joint third position on the approach to three out but gradually edged closer to the pace on the long run to the penultimate fence where he moved to the outside before challenging for the lead. Ridden along upon touching down, the gelding responded well to his jockey and quickened clear along with Jeremy Pass on the run to the last. The pair were stride for stride on the approach to the fence but Giants Table went across his rival's path and unsighted him causing him to fall which left the son of Great Pretender to gallop away to a three-length victory from the staying-on Argumental.

The form looks nothing special, but the unlucky faller has been purchased by Tom Malone and Paul Nicholls for £100,000 at the Cheltenham Festival Sale to run in the colours of John Dance. Giants Table went for a little more when selling to Jamie Codd for £160,000 at the same sale.

A half-brother to point winner Spark To A Flame. His dam is a 2m-2m5f hurdle/chase winner and half-sister to French 1m4f Listed winner Christel Flame.

Giants Table has plenty of size and coped well on the soft ground. His pedigree would suggest he has the speed for shorter distances, but I fully expect him to come into his own when the emphasis is on stamina.

GLYNN
5YR BAY GELDING

TRAINER:	Nicky Henderson
PEDIGREE:	Winged Love – Barnish River (Riverhead)
FORM (P2P):	1 -
OPTIMUM TRIP:	2m +
GOING:	Good to Soft

The Owners Group enjoyed great success with the Nicky Henderson-trained Pentland Hills last term, and they look to have another exciting prospect on their hands with Glynn.

The solid-built son of Winged Love made his debut a winning one for Stuart Crawford at Portrush in late March where he travelled notably well under Ben Crawford before taking up the running at the halfway point. His jumping was accurate and he continued to dominate proceedings as he took the third from home.

Still easily going best on the approach to the second last, he jumped the fence in his stride before sauntering down to the final fence, holding off a strong challenge from the runner-up before popping over in style and scooting up the run-in to record an easy three-length success over the odds-on favourite Brief Ambition, who went on to score by four lengths on his next start and now resides at Fergal O'Brien's yard.

The fifth and seventh home also went on to win, giving the form a strong look.

Glynn, a seventh foal, is a half-brother to Nick Alexander's Craiganboy, a two-time winner up to three miles and also point/bumper winner Ciannte. His dam is an unraced half-sister to a fairly useful 2m-2m4f hurdle/chase winner.

Bought by Highflyer at the Goffs Aintree Sale in March for £85,000, he now enters training with Nicky Henderson who will most likely start him over hurdles, where he could reach a decent level.

An individual with plenty of size and scope.

GRANDADS COTTAGE
4YR CHESTNUT GELDING

TRAINER:	Olly Murphy
PEDIGREE:	Shantou – Sarah's Cottage (Topanoora)
FORM (P2P):	1 -
OPTIMUM TRIP:	2m +
GOING:	Good to Soft

Grandads Cottage looked to have a good deal of quality as he bounded to a comfortable success on his debut at Portrush in late March and is now set to carry the colours of John Hales as he embarks on a career under Rules for Olly Murphy.

The well-related chestnut travelled within his comfort zone as he bided his time in the mid-division before making steady progress to go after the long-time front-runner at the fifth from home. Still hard on the bridle, Rob James took a pull upon touching down over the next before allowing the gelding an inch of rein on the approach to three out where he jumped into the lead.

Without being asked for a serious effort the gelding breezed a length clear on the turn for home before producing a foot-perfect leap at the penultimate fence to land with momentum which he carried forward as he quickened into a commanding lead at the last. A spectacular leap there left victory in no doubt as he was pushed out to the line under hands and heels riding to score by a comfortable six lengths from Kilbrook with a further two and a half lengths to The Bosses Oscar in third.

The runner-up has since been purchased by Jonjo O'Neill for £78,000 whilst the third was second on his next start and has joined Gordon Elliott for £75,000.

Grandads Cottage is a full brother to Super Duty, Howaboutnow, Howaboutnever, Shantung and Superfection, all of whom were effective over trips ranging from two miles right up to 3m2f.

To my eye, he looked rather unfurnished and backward at the Aintree Sale in April, but his race was only five days prior to the sale. Given time to mature and fill out, I'm sure he'll be carrying on the family trend of making an impact under Rules for Olly Murphy who alongside his dad, Aiden, paid £200,000 to take him home.

At no point was Grandads Cottage asked for maximum effort and given his scope and physique he should improve with time.

GRANGECLARE NATIVE
4YR CHESTNUT GELDING

TRAINER:	Gordon Elliott
PEDIGREE:	Shantou – Navaro (Be My Native)
FORM (P2P):	1 -
OPTIMUM TRIP:	2m 4f +
GOING:	Good

Not the most visually impressive winner, but there should be plenty more to come from this well-bred son of Shantou.

Grangeclare Native made his debut for Denis Murphy under the guidance of Jamie Codd at Curraghmore in April where he was sent off at odds of 5/2 in the nine-runner four-year-olds' maiden.

The scopey sort tracked the leaders for the main part of the race before taking closer order with four to jump. He was a little untidy at the third from home and had to be ridden away from the fence but was soon back on the bridle on the long swing into the home straight before being more vigorously ridden to get on terms at the penultimate fence. He produced a nice leap there, but was still a length adrift of the leaders before finding an extra gear on the run to the last, overtaking on the approach before producing a good leap to land running and pulling away on the run to the line to win by a widening two and a half lengths from Unbreakable Bond.

Bought by Margaret O'Toole on behalf of Gordon Elliott for £125,000, the gelding comes from a good family and is a full brother to the Nigel Twiston-Davies-trained Rocco. He is also a half-brother to three winners, including Line Ball (bumper/useful 2m-2m5f hurdle/chase), Smart Exit (2m7f-3m hurdle/chase) and Sin Bin (bumper). His dam is an unraced half-sister to good hurdler Mighty Mogul.

Grangeclare Native appears to have a natural blend of speed and stamina and should be effective over a range of trips.

GUNSIGHT RIDGE
4YR BAY GELDING

TRAINER:	Olly Murphy
PEDIGREE:	Midnight Legend – Grandma Griffiths (Eagle Eyed)
FORM (P2P):	1
OPTIMUM TRIP:	2m +
GOING:	Good

Gunsight Ridge looked an above-average gelding as he led a 10-runner field a merry dance on his debut at Loughrea in May.

Trained by Donnchadh Doyle for the Monbeg Syndicate, the four-year-old took to the front under Rob James and never looked back as he jumped from pillar to post with great accuracy and confidence. James got a breather into him at the halfway point before kicking on again after the fourth from home where he held a five-length advantage and wasn't for stopping over the next two fences, taking them quickly in his stride.

Rounding the turn for home, a couple of rivals got to his quarters, but as soon as his jockey pressed the button, the gelding shot clear in a matter of strides, readily quickening to the last where again he was spring-heeled before scorching up the run-in to win by a comprehensive four lengths with a further five back to the third.

The form is yet to be truly tested, but to the eye this was a magnificent performance by Gunsight Ridge. His enthusiastic way of going teamed with an electric turn of foot was a sight to behold.

A half-brother to the late Willie Mullins-trained point/bumper/2m hurdle winner Earth Mother, his dam showed very little on the Flat and over hurdles.

He should be a force to be reckoned with in bumpers for Olly Murphy.

HEARTBREAK KID
4YR BAY GELDING

TRAINER:	Donald McCain
PEDIGREE:	Getaway – Bella's Bury (Overbury)
FORM (P2P):	1 -
OPTIMUM TRIP:	2m 4f +
GOING:	Soft

Heartbreak Kid bolted up on his debut and could make a big name for himself at Donald McCain's northern base.

The strongly made son of Getaway created a lasting impression when embarking on his racing career in a four-year-olds' maiden at Kirkistown in early March where he travelled and jumped like a dream on the heels of the pacesetters before being produced to lead on the bridle at the third from home.

From there, Barry O'Neill seized the advantage and allowed his mount to up the tempo as they took the penultimate fence before continuing to gallop on relentlessly on the long run to the last. The pair had opened up a commanding lead by the time they had reached the fence and a final foot-perfect leap allowed the gelding to coast up the run-in to record a very easy 30-length success from Kearney Hill, who fell on his next start when looking the likely winner.

Heartbreak Kid appeared to relish the testing soft/heavy ground and looks an absolute bargain for Derek O'Connor and Donald McCain who purchased the gelding at the Goffs Land Rover Store Sale as a three-year-old for the lowly sum of €6,000.

A half-brother to 2m4f-winning hurdler Sonic, who also resides at Bankhouse Stables. His dam showed very little in bumpers and over hurdles but is a sister to 2m5f hurdle winner On Reflection out of a 2m4f-3m1f chase winning half-sister to 2m-3m hurdle/useful chase winner Highfrith.

Set to carry the colours of Tim Leslie, there is plenty to look forward to with this gelding.

HOLD THAT TAUGHT
4YR BAY GELDING

TRAINER:	Venetia Williams
PEDIGREE:	Kayf Tara – Belle Magello (Exit To Nowhere)
FORM (P2P):	1 -
OPTIMUM TRIP:	2m 4f +
GOING:	Soft

★ STAR POTENTIAL ★

This gelding ticks every box.

Hold That Taught is a stoutly bred son of Kayf Tara and will need plenty of time to fully develop into his imposing stature before showing his true potential. However, that didn't stop him being an impressive winner on his debut at Turtulla in a four-year-olds' maiden in March earlier this year.

The pace was strong from the outset in the 13-runner contest, but the bay always looked comfortable as he lolloped along in the middle of the pack before edging a touch closer heading out on to the final circuit. Progress was made to shade third position on the run to four out but a bad blunder cost him valuable ground and caused Simon Cavanagh to become animated in the saddle.

As the pace notably increased on the long run to the next, the gelding regathered his momentum and latched himself on to the leading duo before jumping to the front with a spring-heeled leap over three from home. He continued to be bustled along but responded well to draw a few lengths clear on the approach to the penultimate fence, where again he was far from tidy but he managed to find a leg and land running.

Still cajoled along before the last, a spectacular leap left the race in no doubt and sent him soaring up the run-in to win by a widening 10 lengths from Battle Of Actium who has won since for Colin Bowe.

This was a hugely impressive victory by Hold That Taught, backed up by the clock which recorded a favourable time on the day. Once he hit top gear as the pace increased there was no stopping him and he crossed the line in the manner of a horse with plenty more to give.

From the lovely family of the genuine mare Banjaxed Girl, who was a useful performer for Nigel Twiston-Davies. He is also a half-brother to five winners including Gordon Elliott's Mountain King, Tom George's Gorsky Island, David Pipe's Molo, Nicky Henderson's Comely and La Marianne (dam of winners Ballykan and Maire Banrigh).

Sold as a three-year-old at the prestigious Derby Sale in June 2018 for €70,000, he later went on to make £220,000 when selling to Stroud Coleman Bloodstock and Kate Brazier at the Cheltenham Festival Sale in March. He will now enter training with Venetia Williams.

Natural ability may enable Hold That Taught to win a bumper, or a novice hurdle over the minimum trip, but I fully expect him to show his true potential when the emphasis is on stamina.

IDAS BOY
5YR CHESTNUT GELDING

TRAINER:	Noel Meade
PEDIGREE:	Dubai Destination – Witness Express (Witness Box)
FORM (P2P):	P1 -
OPTIMUM TRIP:	3m +
GOING:	Soft

An imposing individual with a bright future over fences.

Idas Boy pulled up at the penultimate fence on his debut after making steady progress from the rear at Knockanard in February but bounced back at Dromahane in April to win in the manner of a very good horse.

Driving wind and rain made conditions very unpleasant for the Eamonn Gallagher-trained gelding but he didn't let that inconvenience him as he bounded to the front as the flags went up, travelling strongly at the head of affairs before coming back to the field as the gambled-on Dubai Days took up the running.

Confidently ridden by James Hannon, the pair appeared in no rush and bided their time before moving back to the front after the fourth from home where they noticeably upped the tempo and pulled clear on the run to the next. Still hard on the bridle, Idas Boy jumped the fence in his stride and continued to pour on the pressure, stretching his advantage to the best part of six lengths by the time he had reached the penultimate fence where another bold leap allowed him to gallop at leisure down to the last. A final spring-heeled leap sealed the deal, as the pair coasted up the run-in to win by an unextended eight lengths from Jimmil with a further five lengths back to Ballymacaw who has since won a bumper and been placed over hurdles.

By Dubai Destination out of a Witness Box mare, there is very little to speak of in his pedigree, but that didn't stop Margaret O'Toole and Noel Meade splashing out £155,000 to take the gelding home from the Tattersalls Cheltenham Sale in April.

Given his stature, I would imagine it will take time for Idas Boy to reach his full potential. He looks an unrelenting galloper with a liking for soft ground.

IMPERIAL FLEM
4YR BAY GELDING

TRAINER:	Evan Williams
PEDIGREE:	Flemensfirth – Glamorous Leader (Supreme Leader)
FORM (P2P):	2 -
OPTIMUM TRIP:	2m 4f +
GOING:	Soft

Imperial Flem could be a bit of a bargain for trainer Evan Williams.

The son of Flemensfirth appeared to be the second string for Colin Bowe when making his debut at Punchestown's point-to-point track in February and was sent off an unconsidered price of 10/1 under the five-pound claimer Jordan Gainford.

The pair travelled well in the rear of mid-division, but the bay appeared green as the race began to develop and needed to be cajoled along to hold his position at the rear of the group after taking the fourth from home.

He was considerably outjumped at the next but looked to have plenty left in the tank as he made good progress between runners on the run to the penultimate fence which he jumped perfectly before being badly hampered on the landing side by a faller, costing him ground and valuable momentum at a crucial stage.

The leaders had stretched into an unassailable lead on the bend for home, but to this gelding's great credit, he dug deep and found a change of gear as he powered towards the last, jumping it in his stride before scooting up the run-in to grab second place in the dying strides, six lengths behind the winner Power Of Pause.

When taking into account how green Imperial Flem appeared to be, and the amount of ground he lost at the third from home followed by the inconvenience he suffered at the next, it's remarkable he finished so close from such an impossible position.

A full brother to Nigel Twiston-Davies' useful 2m4f hurdle winner Imperial Leader, he is also a half-brother to 2m-2m4f hurdle winner Swantykay. His dam is a bumper winner out of a bumper/2m-2m4f hurdle/chase winner.

Purchased as a foal for €26,000, he then passed through the ring as a three-year-old for €50,000 before being snapped up by his current connections for a modest £40,000.

Maybe he has encountered a few issues that I am not aware of, but based on his debut effort, he is a horse full of potential and one which I imagine would benefit from softer ground judging by his exaggerated knee action.

Spying the gap at Oldcastle

IN TOO DEEP
5YR BAY GELDING

TRAINER:	TBC
PEDIGREE:	Malinas – Cheshire Kat (King's Theatre)
FORM (P2P):	1 -
OPTIMUM TRIP:	2m +
GOING:	Good to Soft

This gelding displayed a potent turn of foot to get off the mark at the first time of asking in a five-year-old geldings' maiden at Belharbour in early February which was run in a time 15 seconds quicker than the day's average.

The Cormac Doyle-trained gelding travelled strongly in behind the leaders as they bypassed five out but an untidy leap at the fourth from home caused his jockey to urge him along for a stride or two upon touching down. Quickly back on an even stride, the gelding made good headway on the wide outside to move into third position before an accurate jump at the next took him into a share of the lead.

Still stride for stride on the sharp turn into the home straight, he got in tight to the penultimate fence but instantly picked up and effortlessly pulled three lengths clear before producing a foot-perfect leap at the last which enabled him to gallop away for a comprehensive five-length victory over When You're Ready.

The form has subsequently worked out well with the runner-up going on to be placed in a bumper for Jonjo O'Neill, whilst the third home scored under Rules in a maiden hurdle at Downpatrick. Kiosk Keith, who filled out fourth position, also boosted the form by winning a point-to-point but sadly lost his life the time after.

In Too Deep is the second foal out of Cheshire Kat who is an unraced sister to 2m4f-3m4f hurdle/chase winner Coolking. She is also a half-sister to the useful 2m4f-2m5f chase winner Stewarts House and bumper/2m4f-3m hurdle/chase winner Supreme Builder.

In Too Deep was withdrawn from Cheltenham's February Sale after sustaining an injury but is one to watch out for when fully fit.

He looks a high-class individual with a deadly turn of foot.

ISRAEL CHAMP
4YR BAY GELDING

TRAINER:	David Pipe
PEDIGREE:	Milan – La Dariska (Take Risks)
FORM (P2P):	1 -
OPTIMUM TRIP:	2m +
GOING:	Good/Soft

☆ **STAR POTENTIAL** ☆

A hugely exciting private purchase to join Pond House.

Israel Champ was unrelenting on the front end at Monksgrange in March, when surging into the lead as the flags went up and jumping with pinpoint accuracy. He still travelled powerfully with a length advantage as the runners took five out, but he was joined at the next before pressing on again to jump the third from home with two lengths in hand.

He continued to dominate proceedings and had the field in trouble on the uphill turn for home where he stretched further clear before sauntering over the final two fences to come home to win by an unextended 12 lengths in the fastest time recorded on the day.

His starting price of 10/1 would suggest the result came as a slight surprise, but this was a performance of the highest calibre. Given the ease of victory, it's unsurprising in this day and age that the rumoured exchange price was around the half a million pound bracket, which is some return for his jockey Harley Dunne who purchased the gelding as a store at the Derby Sale for €38,000.

By Milan out of a Take Risks mare, he should be effective over a trip but his dam is related to a 1m2f Flat winner who later went on to win a Listed hurdle over 2m4f and there are links back to the likes of Aidan O'Brien's Le Brivido. The further family includes Munster National-placed Stellar Notion and Hollywoodien.

This is an imposing, strong, deep-chested gelding and I expect him to follow in the same footsteps as Eden Du Houx who had a similar profile before joining these connections.

IT SURE IS
4YR BAY GELDING

TRAINER:	Nicky Henderson
PEDIGREE:	Shirocco – Stay At Home Mum (Presenting)
FORM (P2P):	1 -
OPTIMUM TRIP:	2m +
GOING:	Good to Soft

It Sure Is looked a useful type as he made his debut in a nine-runner four-year-olds' maiden at Ballynoe in late March.

Despite appearing to be unfancied at odds of 7/1, the gelding was booted to the front as the flags went up where he ensured a good pace and still appeared to be travelling comfortably at the sixth from home. A good jump at the next followed by a foot-perfect leap at four out enabled the son of Shirocco to carry his momentum up the hill towards three from home where despite getting in tight, he managed to quickly regain his stride and continue in the lead.

He ran green on the bend for home and was joined on his outside by the Gigginstown-owned Bloodstone but once straightened up he noticeably increased the pace and landed in the lead over the penultimate fence where his rival made a mistake.

His jockey still hadn't reached for the whip on the approach to the last, but an untidy leap opened the door for Bloodstone but it was quickly closed again when the gelding responded generously to a few sharp reminders and put his head down to score by a cosy half-length with a further 15 back to the third.

Purchased for €48,000 at the prestigious Derby Store Sale, this well-bred individual is out of an unraced sister to the bet365 Chase winner Hennessy, half-sister to the high-class mare Voler La Vedette, hurdle/chase winner Molineaux and Princess Gaia (dam of the highly progressive Good Boy Bobby).

He is now set to join Nicky Henderson after being purchased by David Minton and Anthony Bromley of Highflyer Bloodstock for £150,000.

Personally, I thought It Sure Is looked a little backward as he paraded at Aintree but given that he only ran five days prior to the sale, that's understandable, He also looked physically immature but he had the scope to grow.

Nicky Henderson does very well with the point-to-pointers that come his way and I expect this well-bred sort to thrive for his new connections.

He showed plenty of courage to win and should prove versatile over a range of trips.

JANUARY JETS
5YR BAY GELDING

TRAINER:	Jessica Harrington
PEDIGREE:	Presenting – Poetics Girl (Saddlers' Hall)
FORM (P2P):	F1 -
OPTIMUM TRIP:	2m +
GOING:	Good to Soft

☆ **STAR POTENTIAL** ☆

A very exciting prospect for the novice hurdle division this season.

January Jets made his debut in a competitive maiden won by Chantry House at Tattersalls Farm back in December 2018 where he was in the midst of running a good race until coming to grief with a crunching fall at the penultimate fence.

Given plenty of time to recover, the son of Presenting reappeared at Ballysteen in April earlier this year where he was partnered by Derek O'Connor and sent off the evens favourite of the six-runner five-year-olds' maiden.

The eye was endlessly drawn to the gelding as he travelled with ease in behind the leaders for most of the three miles before a spring-heeled leap carried him into the lead at the fifth from home. Restrained back upon landing, he got in close to the next and forfeited ground, dropping to a close-up fourth on the uphill run to three out.

After a good leap his jockey asked him to pick up, which he did with an electric turn of foot that took him into a challenging position on the approach to the penultimate fence. He landed a length adrift of the leader but picked up impressively on the level and had just nosed in front when producing an almighty leap at the last where his rival exited the race, leaving January Jets to power away to a 10-length success.

This was a very good performance by the five-year-old, who, even without the fall from Ugo Du Misselot, was carrying enough momentum over the last to ensure he would have won.

He comes from a good family and is a full brother to the J P McManus-owned Munster National winner Spider Web. He is also a half-brother to Willie Mullins' smart bumper winner Colreevy, Gordon Elliott's bumper/useful 2m and 2m2f hurdle winner Runfordave and Alan Fleming's 2m-3m hurdle/chase winner Hurricane Darwin.

Sold as a foal for €17,000, he then went through the ring for €55,000 as a three-year-old at the prestigious Derby Sale before being purchased by Brendan Bashford Bloodstock for €115,000 at the Goffs Punchestown Sale in May. He now enters training for Jessica Harrington in the colours of Robcour – owners of Chris's Dream and Impact Factor.

January Jets has all the right components to reach a decent level under Rules and could even develop into a Graded performer.

Jessica Harrington – Gold Cup-winning trainer looking for her next future star

JAVA POINT
4YR BAY GELDING

TRAINER:	Kim Bailey
PEDIGREE:	Stowaway – Classic Sun (Monsun)
FORM (P2P):	U1 -
OPTIMUM TRIP:	2m 4f +
GOING:	Soft

Java Point looks a dour stayer for the midwinter mud.

The good-looking four-year-old got no further than the first fence on his debut at Oldtown back in February when unshipping his jockey but made amends next time at Lismore in a race which only saw three finishers.

Conditions were officially described as soft/heavy, but the field went a good gallop which turned the race into a thorough stamina test. Java Point looked in trouble when pushed along after the fourth from home, but he kept himself within reach of the leaders despite a slow leap at three out and steadily crept into third place before the next.

It was slow-motion stuff on the run to the last, but he found a second wind and was staying on well into second place on the approach to the fence when left in front after the departure of the leader who was four lengths ahead at the time. He had to be kept up to his work on the long run to the line but the runner-up was very leg-weary close home and weakened tamely allowing Java Point to win by 15 lengths.

By Stowaway, his dam is a German 1m2f/Dutch 1m4f winner and is a half-sister to 1m2f-1m4f/2m-2m1f hurdle/chase winner Classic Croco and Listed-placed 7f-12.5f winner Classic Law. The further family link back to African Dancer (third in the Oaks).

Despite his Flat-bias pedigree there is a great deal of stamina on either side of his family and he certainly appeared to have plenty in the reserve tanks at Lismore.

Ed Bailey Bloodstock purchased the gelding for £80,000 at the Cheltenham Festival Sale in March for a new owner at Kim Bailey's yard.

He may have natural speed to win a bumper, but I expect him to flourish over time when upped in trip.

JEREMY PASS
4YR BAY GELDING

TRAINER:	Paul Nicholls
PEDIGREE:	Jeremy – Toulon Pass (Toulon)
FORM (P2P):	F -
OPTIMUM TRIP:	2m +
GOING:	Soft

Jeremy Pass was desperately unlucky to come down at the last when running a big race on his debut at Ballycahane.

The Michael Goff-trained four-year-old was one of nine newcomers when making his debut in the driving snow at the County Limerick track and travelled smoothly in the mid-division before progressing to fourth place after the fifth from home. He continued to hold his position over the next but was considerably outjumped at the third last which forced his jockey to give him the hurry-up for a stride or two upon landing.

The gelding responded well to recover the lost ground and breezed into contention on the home bend before jumping into a share of the lead at the penultimate fence. He started to pull clear with Colin Bowe's Giants Table on the run to the last and around half a length separated the two when his rival veered into his path causing him to be completely unsighted as he came to grief.

It's impossible to say whether he would've been victorious, but he was certainly going as well as the eventual winner and Shane Fitzgerald hadn't gone for everything. Despite the disappointment, there was plenty of promise to take away from the performance, he had jumped brilliantly throughout and showed great battling qualities to get into contention on the home bend.

By Jeremy out of a Toulon mare, he is a half-brother to Warren Greatrex's useful bumper/2m1f-2m5f hurdle winner Knight Pass, 2m hurdle/chase winner Third Opinion and bumper winner Belle Helene. His dam is an unraced half-sister to Grand National winner Monty's Pass and the further family go back to Harbour Pilot, River Wylde and Get Me Out Of Here.

Bought by Paul Nicholls standing alongside Tom Malone for £100,000, the gelding will now run in the colours of John Dance.

He looks well capable of carrying on the family tradition of winning a bumper before embarking on a career over hurdles.

KAKAMORA
4YR BAY GELDING

TRAINER:	Tom George
PEDIGREE:	Great Pretender – Roche D'Or (Rocamadour)
FORM (P2P):	1 -
OPTIMUM TRIP:	2m +
GOING:	Good

Tom George has a yard full of progressive young horses and this well-bred gelding is right up there.

Kakamora was one of four newcomers when making his debut in a strongly contested four-year-olds' maiden at Loughanmore in mid-May but belied any inexperience by going to the front from flag fall to set a strong tempo under Rob James.

The good-looking sort still travelled on the bridle at the fourth from home where he pricked his ears on the approach to the fence and cleared it with plenty of scope before producing a fast leap at the next which gained him a couple of lengths in the air. The tempo started to increase on the run to the penultimate fence, and although he got in a little tight, he managed to land running and maintain his position at the head of affairs.

The field started to stack up behind him on the long swing into the home straight, but despite coming under pressure, the gelding responded generously to his jockey and found an extra gear approaching the last before flicking through the top of the fence and quickening away up the run-in to win by a commanding three lengths from Timberman who stayed on eye-catchingly to finish second.

Purchased by Gerry Hogan Bloodstock for £105,000, he now joins Tom George for successful owner Tim Syder.

Kakamora has a lovely relaxed way of going and appears to be a complete natural over his fences. He is the first foal out of Roche D'Or, an unraced half-sister to the extremely likeable Bitofapuzzle (very useful bumper/2m3f-2m7f hurdle/chase) and Golden Gael (bumper/2m-2m4f hurdle).

He should be well capable of landing a blow in bumpers.

KID COMMANDO
5YR BAY GELDING

TRAINER:	Anthony Honeyball
PEDIGREE:	Robin Des Champs – Banjaxed Girl (King's Theatre)
FORM (P2P):	51 -
OPTIMUM TRIP:	2m +
GOING:	Good to Soft

☆ **STAR POTENTIAL** ☆

An impressive winner on only his second start.

The Peter Flood-trained Kid Commando had a tall reputation when making his debut at Monksgrange in late March, but despite going off the 6/4 favourite the bay never stepped out of mid-division as the race was taken apart by a trailblazing frontrunner and Jamie Codd looked after him to finish fifth.

He reappeared at Quakerstown three weeks later where he put his experience to good use and raced prominently before taking up the running after jumping the sixth from home. He quickly bounded into a three-length advantage by the time he reached the next and continued to maintain that lead before producing another foot-perfect leap at the third last at the top of the hill.

The field were well strung out by that point and the Robin Des Champs gelding wasn't for stopping as he continued with his unrelenting pace on the run to the penultimate fence which he met on a good stride.

From there Kid Commando quickened further clear and entered the home straight on the bridle before another excellent leap at the last sent him soaring up the run-in to win by a very easy 10 lengths from Jack Thunder who has since been snapped up by Charlie Mann after finishing second in a bumper for Pat Doyle.

Kid Commando is the first foal out of the extremely likeable point/bumper/useful 2m-2m5f hurdle/chase winner Banjaxed Girl. She is a half-sister to the useful Mountain King, Gorsky Island and Molo.

Sold at the Punchestown Horses-In-Training Sale in May, Anthony Honeyball secured the winning bid for a reasonable €80,000.

This very likeable sort could make a good impact under Rules where his speed will stand him in good stead in bumpers or the 2m hurdle division.

LARGY FIX
4YR CHESTNUT GELDING

TRAINER:	Noel Meade
PEDIGREE:	Notnowcato – Fix It Lady (Millenary)
FORM (P2P):	F - 1
OPTIMUM TRIP:	2m 4f +
GOING:	Good

☆ STAR POTENTIAL ☆

The Stuart Crawford-trained gelding was never in contention when falling on his debut at Taylorstown at the end of April but was seen in a much greater light three weeks later at Loughanmore when lolloping his way to success.

The flashy white-faced chestnut has a lovely relaxed way of galloping and effortlessly gained ground from the mid-division to move into fourth position at the third from home before advancing a further place when a runner was badly hampered by a faller. He continued to track the two leaders and produced a spring-heeled leap at the next before responding generously for pressure on the long run to the last where he strode into the lead. Another foot-perfect leap there sealed the deal as he lengthened away up the run-in to win by a comfortable four lengths from The Bosses Oscar.

There may have been only two finishers in the race, but Stuart Crawford has introduced the likes of Malone Road and The Very Man to

Loughanmore, and based on this performance, Largy Fix looks another smart graduate from the yard.

Sold at Cheltenham in May, it was Margaret O'Toole who secured the highest bid of £175,000 making the gelding the top lot of the sale. He will now be trained in Ireland by Noel Meade.

Largy Fix is a rangey sort with a long-reaching stride. He may take time to fully come to hand under Rules, but I expect him to have no problem keeping up with a strong pace. Flat tracks and good ground will probably be his ideal conditions, whilst he should come into his own over middle distances.

A very nice individual.

LETS GO CHAMP
4YR BAY GELDING

TRAINER:	Tom George
PEDIGREE:	Jeremy – Dark Mimosa (Bahri)
FORM (P2P):	1
OPTIMUM TRIP:	2m
GOING:	Good

Lets Go Champ looked well above average when digging deep on his debut at Bartlemy in May but he made slightly more than I was expecting when selling to Roger Brookhouse for £375,000 at Doncaster in May.

Sent off the evens favourite of the 10-runner maiden, Rob James always oozed confidence aboard the four-year-old as they tracked the pace in the early stages of the race. A forward move was made on the long run to three from home and Lets Go Champ significantly upped the tempo before producing a foot-perfect leap over the fence.

Pressing on when taking the tight bend for home, he continued to accelerate down to the penultimate fence, which he gave very little respect, but he got away with it and continued to gallop on three lengths clear of the field. That gap was diminished by Full Back at the last who produced a good leap to challenge but Lets Go Champ found extra on the run-in to win by a cosy one-and-a-quarter lengths with a break of 10 lengths back to the third.

Lets Go Champ was tying up a little close home, not helped by his mistake at the last, but he is bred to be suited to trips much sharper than this and so it's credit to his ability that he was able to hold the stoutly bred runner-up at the line.

By Jeremy out of a Bahri mare, the bay is a three-parts brother to Our Conor and a full brother to Joseph O'Brien's bumper winner Scarlet And Dove.

This is a quick sort and I fully expect him to put his potent turn of foot to good use in bumpers before taking to hurdles next season. He enters training with Tom George.

LINELEE KING
4YR GREY GELDING

TRAINER:	Olly Murphy
PEDIGREE:	Martaline – Queen Lee (Lone Bid)
FORM (P2P):	1 -
OPTIMUM TRIP:	2m 4f +
GOING:	Soft

☆ STAR POTENTIAL ☆

A smart-looking French-bred with speed to match his stamina.

Only four went to post in the four-year-olds' maiden at Tinahely in late February but this grey gelding certainly knew his job for the champion point-to-point handler Colin Bowe.

Sent off the 4/5 favourite under Barry O'Neill, the pair took the field along in the early stages but were happy to take a lead and settle into their stride when the others pressed on. Sitting in third at the halfway point but still in touch, the gelding continued to travel strongly and jumped four out with ease before lolloping down the hill to take three from home.

Only three lengths separated the quartet as they set off down the far side, but Linelee King was easily going best and made his move on the wide outside before picking up the running on the bridle as he climbed the hill towards the penultimate fence. Following an accurate leap, the grey quickened on the run to the last and opened up by the best part of five lengths before pinging the fence to draw right away up the home straight and win by an easy eight lengths.

Linelee King was quite clearly in a different parish to his opposition and I liked his easy way of going plus his ability to measure his fences accurately. Tinahely is quite a demanding course which requires stamina to get home, and whilst this gelding obviously stayed the distance well, he also has plenty of speed.

By Martaline out of a Lone Bid mare, his dam was an average Flat performer in France and placed over distances in excess of 1m5f. Her half-sister was a French 2m1f-2m3f hurdle/chase winner out of a 10.5f and 11.5f Flat performer and later 2m-2m5f hurdle/chase winner.

Purchased by Colin Bowe's Milestone Bloodstock for €38,000 as a store horse from the Land Rover Sale in June 2018, he made a healthy return on investment when selling the way of Aiden and Olly Murphy for £160,000 at the Cheltenham Festival Sale in March.

Linelee King looks to have a very bright future.

LOOK ALIVE
5YR BLACK GELDING

TRAINER:	Tom George
PEDIGREE:	Arakan – Itsafamilyaffair (Oscar)
FORM (P2P):	1 -
OPTIMUM TRIP:	2m +
GOING:	Good to Soft

Look Alive created a favourable impression when making all on his debut under James Kenny at Stradbally in April.

The Colin Bowe-trained gelding was the only newcomer in the 11-strong line-up but he belied any inexperience to set a strong tempo from flag fall and bounded into a two-length lead at the third from home before upping the tempo further on the run to the next. His jumping had been a sight to behold throughout and another spring-heeled leap at the penultimate fence allowed him to extend his advantage before popping over the last to stay on admirably under hands and heels riding, holding off the challenge of Lough Har to win by a comfortable three and a half lengths.

The runner-up has since finished in the frame in a bumper and over hurdles for Fergal O'Brien whilst the sixth home went on to win under Rules giving the form a solid look.

Bought by Tom George at Cheltenham's April Sale for the moderate fee of £55,000, the gelding will now run in the same colours of The Big Bite and Singlefarmpayment.

Look Alive is a full brother to Dan Skelton's useful hurdler Ardlethen who won a point in May 2018 before being twice successful over hurdles (2m7f). His dam is an unraced sister to useful 2m-2m4f hurdle/chase winner Baltiman and hurdle winner Drakaina.

This gelding appeared to possess plenty of natural pace, but his pedigree would suggest he will excel when the emphasis is on stamina. He's a very athletic model with plenty of frame to grow into and judging by his jumping ability, he should slot right into a novice hurdle campaign.

MADERA MIST
5YR CHESTNUT MARE

TRAINER:	Tim Vaughan
PEDIGREE:	Stowaway – Odonimee (Idris)
FORM (P2P):	312 -
OPTIMUM TRIP:	2m 4f +
GOING:	Soft

Madera Mist looks very capable of track success when the emphasis is on stamina.

The powerfully made daughter of Stowaway went off a well-supported 7/4 favourite on her debut under Rob James in January at Tyrella but couldn't land a blow on the speed-biased track, where despite making a little headway after the fourth last, she trailed home in third place. It was later reported that she returned home sick.

Given time to recover, she reappeared at Borris House in early March where different tactics were adopted by Jimmy O'Rourke who booted her to the front as the flags went up and set a strong pace. She jumped far better with daylight around her and still travelled strongly when pressed for the lead down the back straight towards three from home. A good jump there allowed her to maintain her position as she upped the ante on the downhill part of the track before pulling a few lengths clear on the approach to the penultimate fence.

Foot perfect again, she landed running and had the measure of the two rivals in behind her when producing an almighty leap at the last which sealed the deal as she stretched right away to win by a comprehensive four lengths from Bannixtown Glory who went on to win a point-to-point by 18 lengths before being successful under Rules for Donald McCain. The third also won next time.

Following her victory, Madera Mist stepped up in grade to compete in a 'winner of two' point-to-point at Portrush where she finished second to Royal Drumlee who has subsequently won again by eight lengths. Back under Rob James, she adopted the tactics that had served her well at Borris House but she forfeited her lead with a slow leap at the last before rallying towards the line.

She's quite a scopey sort for a first foal and her dam was a useful 2m-2m1f hurdle/chase winner. She is a half-sister to 2m3f-3m1f hurdle/chase winner A Decent Excuse out of an unraced granddaughter of Thyestes Chase winner Tarthistle.

Snapped up by Select Racing Bloodstock on behalf of Tim Vaughan for £40,000, there should be plenty of races to be won with her especially on a galloping track with plenty of give underfoot.

MAKE ME A BELIEVER
4YR BAY GELDING

TRAINER:	David Pipe
PEDIGREE:	Presenting – Kiltiernan Robin (Robin Des Champs)
FORM (P2P):	F -
OPTIMUM TRIP:	2m +
GOING:	Soft

David Pipe has a strong team of horses for the coming season and Make Me A Believer is one worth following.

The well-bred son of Presenting only faced three rivals when making his debut for Colin Bowe in a four-year-olds' maiden at Ballyarthur in mid March, but the standard appeared strong and he didn't go unnoticed in the market.

Ridden by Barry O'Neill in the colours of the Milestone Racing Partnership, the pair tracked the leaders for the main part of the race before advancing into second spot at the fifth from home. The gelding still travelled strongly under his motionless jockey as they took four out and gradually inched closer to the pace setter on the uphill section of the track. Asked to see a stride on the approach to the third from home, Make Me A Believer responded and instantly quickened into the wings, producing an almighty leap which saw him gain several lengths on the leader who made a slight mistake. Unfortunately, the gelding's race ended there as he couldn't quite get out the landing gear and crumpled a stride after the fence.

How he would've fared if he had stood up is impossible to say, but he was still travelling very strongly at the time and the manner with which he picked up once asked for an effort suggested he had plenty more to give.

A half-brother to the highly regarded dual bumper winner King Roland. His dam is an unraced half-sister to French/Belgian 2m1f-2m7f chase winner Brise Du Large.

This exciting individual has now joined David Pipe at Pond House and there's plenty to suggest he can have a fruitful career. He looks to possess plenty of size but should easily make his presence known in bumpers before progressing to hurdles.

MEYER LANSKY
4YR BAY GELDING

TRAINER:	Jonjo O'Neill
PEDIGREE:	Mahler – Sea Breeze Lady (Oscar)
FORM (P2P):	3 -
OPTIMUM TRIP:	2m +
GOING:	Good to Soft

Meyer Lansky looked a work-in-progress when making his debut in a highly competitive four-year-olds' maiden at Liscarroll in March.

Matt Collins' gelding travelled strongly, if not a little keenly, as he tracked the pacesetters through the race but still appeared to be going well after taking the fourth from home. On the downhill section three from home, he seemed a little unbalanced and changed his legs a couple of times before carrying his head awkwardly. He jumped the fence well and found an extra gear on the landing side but continued to run ungainly and hopped the path before moving into fourth place.

He got close to the penultimate fence but quickly found his feet and moved into third before attempting to close on the leaders who had shot six lengths clear. He responded well to pressure and pulled away from the horses in behind, but he couldn't gain on those in front and travelled home to secure third, nine lengths behind Papa Tango Charly and Big Bresil.

This was a strong maiden. The winner has since gone on to fetch a record-breaking sum of £440,000 at the Aintree Sale in April whilst the runner-up sold the way of Roger Brookhouse for £170,000. This gelding also sold at the Grand National Sale to Jonjo O'Neill for £100,000.

A half-brother to point winner Dramatic Approach, who ran well in a bumper for Neil Mulholland and featured in last year's book. His dam is an unraced sister to bumper/2m5f-3m2f hurdle/chase winner/National second Oscar Time.

This is a good-looking type with plenty of strength to his frame. Given how green he ran, he should come on considerably with experience and is one to look forward to.

MINELLA TARA
4YR BAY GELDING

TRAINER:	Fergal O'Brien
PEDIGREE:	Kayf Tara – Jolie Landaise (Beaudelaire)
FORM (P2P):	F -
OPTIMUM TRIP:	2m +
GOING:	Soft

Minella Tara shaped well on his debut at Stowlin in May until departing at the last when still holding every chance.

The John Nallen-trained gelding travelled strongly throughout the four-year-olds' maiden and was still going well at the fifth from home where he gained momentum with an accurate leap to carry him into a share of third position. He stuttered into the next but was quick on the landing side and moved into second place before brushing through the top of three out as the pace increased.

Around half a length separated him from Colin Bowe's Don Diablo as they swung the bend towards the penultimate fence, where a good leap enabled the gelding to take charge before increasing the tempo on the run to the last. Trapped wide, he forfeited ground approaching the fence and was around a length down when he overjumped and crashed out of the race.

Whether he would have gone on to win is open to debate, but the son of Kayf Tara showed ability to that point to suggest he should have a fruitful career under Rules for his new trainer Fergal O'Brien, who purchased the gelding at the Doncaster Sale in May for £90,000.

Closely related to I'm All You Need, a 2m hurdle/2m4f chase winner for Paul Nolan, and bumper winner Owenacurra Lass. He is also a half-brother to bumper winner Mercury Bay. His dam is an unraced half-sister to 1m4f Flat/high-class 2m-2m3f jumper winner Bilboa.

Minella Tara should prove successful in bumpers for a yard who have an excellent strike rate in that sphere, before going on to better things.

MINELLA TRUMP
5YR BAY GELDING

TRAINER:	Donald McCain
PEDIGREE:	Shantou – One Theatre (King's Theatre)
FORM (P2P):	1 -
OPTIMUM TRIP:	2m 4f +
GOING:	Soft

A useful-looking recruit for Donald McCain.

Minella Trump made his debut in appalling weather conditions at Ballycahane at the beginning of March in what looked to be a well-contested five-year-olds' maiden.

The bay jumped and travelled smoothly throughout and was around five lengths behind the leader as they approached four from home, where he got a little close. Very little momentum was lost as he made his move to go after the pacesetter before three out where a good leap enabled him to land one length adrift. He continued to sit and pressure his rival on the long swing into the home straight before joining him in the air as they took the penultimate fence.

Once given the hurry-up on the landing side the gelding responded generously and soon pulled a few lengths clear before coming up well for the last to stay on stoutly to the line to win by six lengths from the more experienced Oscarsman with a further 20 lengths back to Woddy Wynne.

The five-year-old left the impression he was given a considerate ride and was value for more than the winning margin. Johnny Barry was motionless for most of the race and only had to administer a few sharp cracks between the final two fences before pushing out to the line under hands and heels riding in a race which clocked a good time on the day.

When I saw him at the Aintree Sale in April, he looked a little immature and lacked the size of some of the others on parade, which is a possible reason for him selling for only £90,000 – a relatively cheap price in comparison to others sold on the day.

By Shantou out of a King's Theatre mare, he is bred to stay, and his family were mostly effective over trips in excess of two and a half miles.

Given his age, he will most likely start over hurdles where he could come into his own in the midwinter mud.

MOORE CLOUDS
4YR GREY FILLY

TRAINER:	TBC
PEDIGREE:	Cloudings – Wednesday Girl (Rudimentary)
FORM (P2P):	1 -
OPTIMUM TRIP:	2m +
GOING:	Soft/Heavy

A lovely daughter of Cloudings from the family of Many Clouds.

Peter Flood's four-year-old made her debut in an 11-runner maiden at Durrow in March in an incident-packed race which saw only five finishers but clocked a time 14 seconds quicker than average.

Moore Clouds managed to steer clear of any casualties as she took the field along at an unrelenting tempo, which had many of her opposition out of their comfort zones from an early stage. She was a little keen but still held a comfortable two-length advantage as she quickly went from A to B over four from home before scooting up the hill to three out where again she was very efficient.

She increased the pace further upon touching down where only Imperial View could find the gears to go after her, but despite getting in close to the penultimate fence, Moore Clouds quickly regathered her momentum before producing a foot-perfect leap at the last to propel her up the run-in to win by a cosy two and a half lengths.

Following the race, her trainer said she is a great jumper and had been working well at home. He also added the filly had loved everything she had done ever since day one.

There wasn't much to her when she sold through the ring at the Grand National Aintree Sale in April. She's a petite model, but well balanced with

JODIE STANDING'S POINT-TO-POINT RECRUITS 2019/20

a good shoulder and sold the way of Highflyer Bloodstock for a modest £56,000. Unfortunately, following the sale, the filly went intermittently lame and has been returned to her previous handler's base.

Closely related to Richard Hobson's point/2m3f hurdle winner Going Gold. Her dam placed in a point and is a half-sister to 3m/3m2f chase winner Kings Eclipse out of a half-sister to bumper/2m4f-3m hurdle/chase winner Ballyvooney. From the family of Many Clouds.

Moore Clouds has bags of speed which will see her go well in bumpers. Hopefully she can overcome her setbacks and return to the track fully sound.

MOSSY FEN
4YR BAY GELDING

TRAINER:	Nigel Twiston-Davies
PEDIGREE:	Milan – Inch Native (Supreme Leader)
FORM (P2P):	F1 -
OPTIMUM TRIP:	2m 4f +
GOING:	Soft

Mossy Fen got no further than the first fence when embarking on his pointing career in early April at Castletown-Geoghegan but atoned for that mistake the following weekend at Loughbrickland where he stayed on gamely up the home straight to land the spoils.

The pace was a fair one from the outset in the 11-runner maiden due to a trailblazing front runner, but James Walsh was happy to bide his time and allow the gelding to settle into a rhythm before making his move.

Once jumping the fifth from home, the pack began to close on the long-time leader and quickly swallowed him up on the landing side of four out where this gelding moved into fourth position. The pace increased on the quick run to the next and although Mossy Fen produced a good leap, he was caught a little flat-footed upon touching down when the front two pressed on up the hill.

After a few sharp reminders, the gelding found top stride and stayed on strongly to take second position before turning the bend for home. With momentum carrying him forward he flew over the last and continued to eat into the leader's advantage before finding an extra gear to overtake close home and win going away.

Somptueux, who was two lengths back in second, has since joined Henry De Bromhead for £70,000, whilst Clondaw Pretender, who was 14 lengths third, went on to fill out the same position next time. The fourth home, Deluxe Range, is now with Sandy Thomson after selling through the ring for £17,000.

Loughbrickland is a tight, seven-furlong circuit which probably wouldn't be ideal for this rangey-looking individual. He will be seen in a much greater light on a stiffer track where he can really use his lengthy stride.

Bought by Carl Hinchy and Willy Twiston-Davies at Cheltenham's Aintree Sale, he will enter the training ranks with his dad, Nigel, at Grange Hill Farm.

By Milan out of a Supreme Leader mare and related to the high-class 2m-2m4f chaser, Sound Man.

Mossy Fen is a horse for the future.

MUSTANG ALPHA
4YR BAY GELDING

TRAINER:	Jamie Snowden
PEDIGREE:	Stowaway – Tupia (Hernando)
FORM (P2P):	1
OPTIMUM TRIP:	2m +
GOING:	Good

This son of Stowaway displayed a high cruising speed and potent turn of foot to win a four-year-olds' maiden at Bartlemy in mid-May.

Mustang Alpha was one of six newcomers in the 11-runner contest and was happy to take a tow into the race as he travelled with ease under Shane Fitzgerald in behind the leaders who set a good pace. Still going well in a close-up sixth at the third from home, the gelding saw a stride and improved his position to fourth place before saving ground and nipping up the inside on the tight bend for home.

Encouraged to see a stride on the approach to the penultimate fence, the gelding took off and produced an almighty leap, allowing him to land with momentum which carried him to the front on the run to the last. Another foot-perfect jump there sealed the deal as he went scorching up the run-in to win by a widening six lengths with a further eight back to the third.

The distance of ground this gelding managed to put between himself and the field in a matter of strides was sublime and can only bode well for when he is contesting races over a shorter distance under Rules for Jamie Snowden who purchased the gelding for £135,000 at the Goffs Sale at Doncaster in May on behalf of Mrs Carolyn Kendrick.

The immediate family have been disappointing, but his dam was a winner in France over 12.5f and she was a half-sister to the high-class Noland. The further family stretch back to Bosra Sham and Hector Protector.

Jamie Snowden does very well with his horses and this one could take high rank amongst his bumper performers.

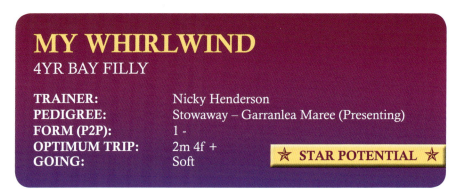

All eyes will be on this mare when she makes her debut.

My Whirlwind certainly whipped up a storm in the sales ring at the Cheltenham Festival Sale in March when selling to Tattersalls Ireland Chief Executive Matt Mitchell who took a telephone bid from Nicky Henderson for £400,000 – a record price for a point-to-point mare sold at public auction.

The well-related daughter of Stowaway was unrelenting on the front end as she embarked on her debut in the four-year-old mares' maiden at Ballycahane which saw Posh Trish emerge victorious two years ago. The weather was atrocious, but she splashed her way through the puddles and was still hard on the bridle as she sailed over four out where she held a two-length advantage.

She got in a little close to the next and the field began to close but as soon as Declan Lavery asked her to extend, she responded generously and reasserted her advantage with a good leap at the penultimate fence. From there she doubled her advantage and a further good jump at the last saw her romp away to victory without being asked too many questions to record the fastest time set on the day.

My Whirlwind is an imposing mare whose dam is a full sister to the useful chaser Sizing Coal and also a half-sister to useful bumper/2m3f hurdle/2m5f chase winner Whatwillwecallher. The further family go back to Albertas Run.

Nicky Henderson does exceptionally well with the mares, and this looks an exciting prospect to go to town with this season.

NOREEN BAWN
4YR BAY FILLY

TRAINER:	Barry Connell
PEDIGREE:	Jeremy - Rose N Alice (Anshan)
FORM (P2P):	2
OPTIMUM TRIP:	2m +
GOING:	Good

★ STAR POTENTIAL ★

Noreen Bawn was first past the post on her debut at Dromahane in April but was demoted to second due to causing interference on the run to the last.

The daughter of Jeremy travelled enthusiastically behind the leaders for most of the three miles and was still hard on the bridle as the field sailed over four from home. She continued to catch the eye on the run to the next where she was quick in the air before being asked to take closer order on the run to the penultimate fence. Responding well, the filly pricked her ears and accelerated into the wings of the fence and jumped nimbly to land with a length advantage.

She was readily extending her lead as she continued to quicken en route to the last but something appeared to spook her in the crowd which sent her veering off to her right causing interference with Tucanae who was attempting to rally in behind. Her jockey soon had her straightened up and they jumped the fence accurately before fighting gamely up the run-in to score by a neck.

To my eye, without the benefit of the head-on view, the filly hadn't appeared to improve her placing with the incident, but connections were unsuccessful in their appeal. Nevertheless, this was a quality performance by Noreen Bawn. She was easily travelling best throughout the contest and clearly has a potent turn of foot at her disposal.

Purchased by Gerry Hogan Bloodstock at the Punchestown Sale in May for €220,000 she will now be trained by Barry Connell, who is set to take out his own trainer's licence in the new year. She may run under the name of Keith Black in the meantime.

Well related, she is a half-sister to 2m hurdle winner Cotton Jenny. Her dam won over 2m as a chaser and is a full sister to 2m chase/2m4f hurdle winner Captain Dash. The further family link back to high-class chaser up to 3m1f Simply Dashing.

Noreen Bawn looks a classy sort with bags of speed.

OFFTHESHOULDER
5YR BAY GELDING

TRAINER:	Lucinda Russell
PEDIGREE:	Gold Well – Zafilly (Zafonic)
FORM (P2P):	1 -
OPTIMUM TRIP:	2m 4f +
GOING:	Soft

Offtheshoulder looks a sure-fire winner for Lucinda Russell.

The scopey son of Gold Well displayed a very willing and gritty attitude on his debut at Cragmore in February when rallying tenaciously after the last to win by a length from the well-supported 7/4 favourite, Oscar Robertson.

The Sean Doyle-trained newcomer looked very accomplished in the jumping department and caught the eye with his relaxed way of travelling on the heels of the leaders for the majority of the three miles. He still moved stylishly in third place over three from home and responded well for gentle pressure from Barry O'Neill to move into second position on the uphill climb to the next. He was a touch clumsy there which cost him a length, but he was soon picked up by his jockey and gathered plenty of momentum on the run to the last, where he met the fence on a good stride to join the leader in the air before asserting under a strong drive on the run to the line, winning with a little up his sleeve.

Offtheshoulder hails from a successful family and is closely related to three point winners. He is also a half-brother to bumper/2m hurdler Tangled Web and bumper winner Kennady. His dam placed on the Flat and is a half-sister to 1m4f Group 2 winner Rifapour and very smart hurdler Tiger Groom.

The five-year-old is a tall gelding and was highly recommended to Lucinda Russell by his previous trainer. Despite his size, he is a very athletic type with an impressive stride. He should be more than capable of notching up a sequence over hurdles before embarking on a fruitful chase campaign in time.

A horse with a definite future.

ON THE BANDWAGON
4YR BAY GELDING

TRAINER:	Jonjo O'Neill
PEDIGREE:	Oscar – Deep Supreme (Supreme Leader)
FORM (P2P):	2 -
OPTIMUM TRIP:	2m 4f +
GOING:	Soft

The Denis Murphy-trained son of Oscar made his debut at Monksgrange in late March where he shaped with great promise to finish second, staying on in eye-catching style in a race won by the highly regarded Israel Champ.

The pace was strong from the outset and Jamie Codd was intent on giving his mount a patient ride as he held him up in the early stages before making steady progress down the back straight, jumping into a share of fourth position at the fifth from home before enhancing his place further at the next. He stayed on into third on the uphill run towards the bend for home and responded well to a shake of the reins to move into second place between the final two fences before pulling clear of the remainder on the run to the line – 12 lengths adrift of the winner.

It was clear from an early stage that Israel Champ was not for being caught, but there was nothing but encouragement to be taken from the way On The Bandwagon crept into the race to secure second position without being asked too many questions.

By Oscar out of a Supreme Leader mare, he is a half-brother to David Pipe's bumper/useful 2m-2m3f hurdler Heath Hunter and Dan Skelton's 2m3f/2m4f chase winner Pretty Reckless. His dam is an unraced sister to high-class 2m5f-3m chaser Nick Dundee and a half-sister to high-class 2m hurdler Ned Kelly.

Purchased by Stroud Coleman acting on behalf of Jonjo O'Neill at the Goffs Aintree Sale in April for £160,000. The gelding is now set to carry the colours of Martin Broughton & Friends who owned the likes of the ill-fated Taquin Du Seuil with Jonjo, as well as Dodging Bullets and more recently Quel Destin with Paul Nicholls.

On The Bandwagon looks a useful type with a natural ability for jumping. He should have enough speed for a bumper but he's a smooth traveller and I'd expect him to thrive over hurdles once upped in trip.

Jamie Codd – a master in the saddle

PAPA TANGO CHARLY
4YR CHESTNUT GELDING

TRAINER:	Jonjo O'Neill
PEDIGREE:	No Risk At All – Chere Elenn (Mansonnien)
FORM (P2P):	1 -
OPTIMUM TRIP:	2m 4f +
GOING:	Soft

☆ **STAR POTENTIAL** ☆

A hugely exciting individual with a tall reputation.

Papa Tango Charly broke the record for a point-to-point gelding sold at Aintree's Grand National Sale in April when going under the hammer for £440,000, selling the way of Aidan Kennedy and Jonjo O'Neill who outbid J P McManus. He will now run in the colours of Martin Tedham – the CEO of Wasdell Group and the new sponsor to Jackdaws Castle.

In this day and age it's unsurprising to see a rising star make that sort of sum, especially given the impression he left when lolloping his way to success on his pointing debut at Liscarroll back in March.

The eye-filling chestnut always travelled effortlessly under Barry O'Neill in a share of the lead and moved stylishly to the front over the third from home before considerably upping the ante with the minimal amount of fuss on the run to the next. He jumped the fence in his stride but had to be ridden along upon touching down and was momentarily joined for the lead by Big Bresil, before reasserting his advantage on the turn for home.

Nursed around the bend by his jockey, Papa Tango Charly used his ground-eating stride to put daylight between himself and his rival, turning into the home straight with a healthy advantage before popping over the last and extending up the run-in to win by four lengths.

This had the look of a strong maiden and the runner-up has since been sold for £170,000 to Roger Brookhouse whilst the third is now with Jonjo O'Neill after selling for £105,000 to Stroud Coleman.

Papa Tango Charly doesn't boast the strongest pedigree. His dam placed over hurdles up to 2m3f and is a half-sister to 3m-3m2f hurdle/chase winner Jupiter Rex out of a French 2m1f-3m chase winning half-sister to 2m1f-2m7f hurdle/chase winner/Grand National second Encore Un Peu.

At no point was the gelding asked for maximum effort to win his point and hopes are high that he can go right to the very top for his new connections.

PENS MAN
4YR CHESTNUT GELDING

TRAINER:	Jonjo O'Neill
PEDIGREE:	Sholokhov – Dudeen (Anshan)
FORM (P2P):	1 -
OPTIMUM TRIP:	2m +
GOING:	Good

There was so much to like about Pens Man's success at Lisronagh at the end of March.

The Sam Curling-trained chestnut travelled with tremendous exuberance in a share of the lead and his natural athleticism at his fences was a sight to behold. Pat King took a pull as the gelding sailed over five and four out before allowing him to press on as he approached the third from home. He was a little untidy there and had to be ridden along on the landing side, but soon bounded back to the front before a fluent leap at the penultimate fence handed him a length advantage.

King got a little more vigorous in the saddle on the turn into the straight and issued a couple of cracks behind the saddle, which was met with an instant response from the gelding who quickened further clear before producing another foot-assured leap over the last, allowing him to gallop up the run-in to win by a comfortable two lengths from Colin Bowe's Royal Crown.

The form looks strong. Face The Odds, who was third, won next time by five lengths and was subsequently sold to Margaret O'Toole and Noel Meade for £165,000, whilst Royal Crown now resides at Colin Tizzard's yard having been purchased for £110,000 at the Goffs Aintree Sale.

Pens Man was purchased at the same sale for what looks to be a good price of £82,000 by Stroud Coleman standing alongside Jonjo O'Neill. The gelding is a good size and an athletic walker which translates to his races.

The flashy chestnut is closely related to the Philip Hobbs-trained Catherines Well who won over hurdles and is a half-brother to point-to-point winner Hurlstone Point, Neville, Parthian Empire and Oyster Perch.

The four-year-old may not prove to be a world-beater, but his smooth way of travelling and natural jumping ability will stand him in good stead for winning races. I imagine him to be suited to good ground.

PICANHA
5YR BROWN GELDING

TRAINER:	Richard Phillips
PEDIGREE:	Malinas – Royal Bride (Kayf Tara)
FORM (P2P):	1 -
OPTIMUM TRIP:	2m 4f +
GOING:	Good

Picanha has the potential to develop into a useful performer for Richard Phillips.

The imposing five-year-old made his debut at Moig South in November last year and jumped impressively on the heels of the leader throughout the contest before moving closer to challenge at the fifth from home. From there, the race turned into a duel as he and Defuture Is Bright – in receipt of 10lbs, after his jockey's claim – went toe-to-toe over the next few fences where neither gave an inch as they continually upped the pace. On the bend for home, Picanha slightly lost out by travelling widest, but to his great credit he found the courage to battle and despite being narrowly outjumped at the last he responded valiantly to Jimmy O'Rourke's urgings to get up in the shadows of the post and win by a short head.

This truly was an impressive performance backed up by the clock which recorded the fastest time of the day. The runner-up is now with Christian Williams having placed again, whilst the third has placed twice in a maiden hurdle for Denis Hogan.

Half-brother to a point winner, his dam is an unraced sister to bumper/2m-3m2f hurdle/very useful chase winner The Package and 2m3f hurdle winner Bound Hill.

Picanha was purchased at Cheltenham in November by Tom Malone for £110,000 and has since gone into training with Richard Phillips where he has undergone plenty of strengthening and conditioning work.

He is a horse who will need plenty of time to fully develop into his sizeable frame, but the raw ability is there for him to reach a decent level.

POWER OF PAUSE
4YR CHESTNUT GELDING

TRAINER:	Willie Mullins
PEDIGREE:	Doyen – Shady Pines (Great Palm)
FORM (P2P):	1 -
OPTIMUM TRIP:	2m +
GOING:	Good

This gelding has the speed to contest bumpers or the two-mile novice hurdle division.

Power Of Pause made a convincing winning debut in a 2m4f maiden point-to-point at Punchestown in February for trainer/jockey combo Patrick Turley and Mark O'Hare who jointly purchased the gelding at the Goffs Land Rover Store Sale in June 2018 for €28,000.

The four-year-old bided his time in the mid-division and always looked in control despite being pushed along for a stride or two after jumping the fifth from home. He was soon back on the bridle and made a position entering the back straight before jumping the fourth last with plenty of scope.

The eye was drawn to the gelding as he made progress through the field on the run to three out where again he was foot perfect and touched down in fourth position before gaining a further place on the turn for the home straight. A big jump at the penultimate fence gave him momentum to tackle the leaders and it wasn't long before he poked his nose in front before quickening away in style to jump the last with a four-length advantage which stretched to six by the time he had crossed the line.

O'Hare recommended the chestnut to Harold Kirk and it was he who purchased the gelding for a sum of £180,000 at the Cheltenham Festival Sale in March for trainer Willie Mullins.

He does not look the scopiest of individuals but his athleticism and the way he skipped through his race before producing a turn of foot is sure to stand him in good stead when contesting bumpers or novice hurdles over the minimum trip. A theory backed up by his pedigree.

His family is packed with speed, including his dam who won over two miles as a hurdler. She herself was a half-sister to eight winners, including Hard Shoulder (1m Flat/2m hurdle), Mccracken (1m5f-2m Flat and 2m3f hurdle/chase) and Islandmagee (2m-2m2f hurdle/chase). The further family link back to a 1m2f Flat winner and later 2m hurdle winner.

Power Of Pause could be one of the yard's leading bumper horses this term.

RAMILLIES
4YR GREY GELDING

TRAINER:	Willie Mullins
PEDIGREE:	Shantou – Mrs Wallensky (Roselier)
FORM (P2P):	1 -
OPTIMUM TRIP:	2m +
GOING:	Soft

Ramillies joins Willie Mullins having impressed in an English point-to-point.

The good-looking grey made his debut for Sophie Lacey in the colours of her husband, Tom, at East Devon's Bishops Court track where 14 runners went to post on ground described as soft, heavy in places following the onslaught of Storm Freya.

The gelding travelled strongly throughout the three-mile contest under the excellent Tommie O'Brien and moved into fourth position after taking five out. He continued to make his way through the field on the way to the next where a good jump enabled him to touch down in second place before a further spring-heeled leap at the next gained him a length or two in the air.

He was still hard on the bridle as the field climbed their way to the penultimate fence and despite landing steeply the gelding quickened stylishly on the level before breezing his way to the front. He held a healthy lead as he popped over the last where although he ran a little green a few strides after the fence, once he straightened up, he powered through the line to record an easy five-length success.

Following the race Tom Lacey described the gelding as "still very raw" but the manner with which he put the race to bed was indicative of a horse with a big future under Rules. Willie Mullins, who has purchased the likes of Blackbow from Cottage Field Stables, obviously liked what he saw and was prepared to pay £215,000 to take him home from the Cheltenham Festival Sale.

Ramillies is a half-brother to Laura Mongan's 2m4f chase winner Miss Yeats, Nick Alexander's point winner Manetti and Moonlit Theatre who finished second three times from four starts. His dam is a bumper/2m4f and 2m6f hurdle winner (also placed at Graded level) and is a half-sister to bumper/2m6f hurdle winner Ballyguider Bridge.

There is plenty of stamina in this pedigree, but he showed a potent turn of foot which may encourage connections to give him a go in a bumper before sending him over the sticks.

RIVER TYNE
4YR BAY FILLY

TRAINER:	TBC
PEDIGREE:	Geordieland – Not Now Nellie (Saddlers' Hall)
FORM (P2P):	1 -
OPTIMUM TRIP:	2m +
GOING:	Soft

River Tyne could look well bought by Ryan Mahon for £50,000.

The daughter of Geordieland made her winning debut in deteriorating conditions at Turtulla in March where she clocked the second fastest time of the day when getting up to win by a cosy two lengths.

Pat King did well to survive a terrible blunder at the fourth from home when sitting in a share of second place, but the filly soon recovered her position before taking the next, where she was much neater. Pushed along approaching two from home, she responded well and jumped accurately to take up the lead before slightly running down the last where she still held a narrow advantage. Headed momentarily on the landing side she rallied tenaciously and found an extra gear before being handed the race when her rival hung badly to their left on the run to the line.

The way River Tyne responded once given the hurry-up suggested she won with a little bit up her sleeve. The form also received a boost when the second went on to win and has since joined Donald McCain. The sixth, Doin'whatshelikes also ran well to be second on her next start and is now with Paul Nicholls having switched hands for £82,000.

River Tyne is a half-sister to David Pipe's bumper/2m-3m hurdle/chase winner Close House and the extended family link back to the likes of Morley Street and Granville Again.

She showed enough speed to be effective over the minimum trip but will come into her own over further.

ROYAL CROWN
4YR CHESTNUT GELDING

TRAINER:	Colin Tizzard
PEDIGREE:	Creachadoir – Royal Army (Pirate Army)
FORM (P2P):	2 -
OPTIMUM TRIP:	2m
GOING:	Good to Soft

A sharp-looking type.

Royal Crown came up against Pens Man on his debut at Lisronagh at the end of March and fought bravely until his stamina gave way in the latter stages.

The Colin Bowe-trained gelding set a good early pace and was still to the fore on the run to five out where he was joined in the air on either side after a tardy leap. Nudged along for a stride or two he soon recovered the lost ground and pressed on with the eventual winner going to four from home. The pair were locked together over the next before opening up on the field as they swung the bend towards the final two fences.

A half-length separated the two as they sailed over the penultimate fence with Pens Man touching down with the momentum after a better leap. Although firmly ridden, Royal Crown kept responding generously but his stamina appeared to peter out on the run to the last where he dropped a couple of lengths off the leader. A blunder at the final fence didn't help his cause but he picked up well and was readily holding second position at the line.

Speedily bred, the gelding is a half-brother to three winners including the 8.5f German Listed-placed Ripley and Listed winner Romanoff who was successful up to 1m4f in Switzerland. His dam was also successful on the Flat in Germany.

Royal Crown appeared to be limited in size at the Aintree Sale in April, but that didn't stop Colin Tizzard forking out £110,000 to take him home.

Bumpers or novice hurdles over the minimum distance will be his forte this season. He could be hard to catch with his speed on the front end.

SKATMAN
4YR BROWN GELDING

TRAINER:	Paul Nicholls
PEDIGREE:	Mustameet – Maid For Action (Alderbrook)
FORM (P2P):	1
OPTIMUM TRIP:	2m +
GOING:	Good

Skatman may not boast the strongest of pedigrees but he left a lasting impression when making a winning debut.

The son of Mustameet announced himself on to the racing scene at Dromahane's top pointing track back in late April where he faced a total of 11 rivals in the four-year-olds' maiden. Despite a seemingly unfancied starting price of 6/1, Barry Stone gave the gelding a cool, confident ride and were probably value for more than the two-length winning distance.

Skatman was held up in the early stages but steadily crept into contention as the race developed and had eased into a close-up ninth at the fifth from home. He continued to make stylish progress on the approach to the next where he touched down in third before gaining a further position as the pace cranked up a notch on the bend before three from home.

The gelding slightly pecked on landing there, but soon picked up and quickened on the bridle to move alongside the leader before jumping to the front over the penultimate fence. Coaxed along on the landing side, he drew a length clear before pricking his ears and easing into the last. Barbados Buck's attempted to stage a rally but once over the fence this gelding stuck his head down and rallied gamely to win in comprehensive style.

Tom Malone and Paul Nicholls were responsible for purchasing the gelding at the Doncaster May Sale for £170,000 to run in the colours of Chris Giles. The pair also bought the runner-up a few weeks earlier at Punchestown for €210,000 and he will run in the colours of Andy Stewart.

Skatman looks a big-framed individual who may take time to come to hand. He's not short of pace and could quite easily contest a spring bumper but connections may send him straight over hurdles.

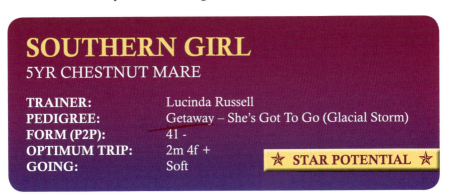

SOUTHERN GIRL
5YR CHESTNUT MARE

TRAINER:	Lucinda Russell
PEDIGREE:	Getaway – She's Got To Go (Glacial Storm)
FORM (P2P):	41 -
OPTIMUM TRIP:	2m 4f +
GOING:	Soft

☆ STAR POTENTIAL ☆

Southern Girl looks an above-average mare and an exciting addition to Lucinda Russell's yard.

The well-bred daughter of Getaway possibly lacked race fitness when filling out fourth place on her debut in a strong mares' maiden at Kilfeacle in January. Given time to mature, she reappeared in late April at Quakerstown where expectations were obviously high as she was heavily supported into 4/5 favourite under Derek O'Connor.

Waited with in mid-division, the pair moved closer with a good jump at the fourth from home and progressed into third with another good leap at the fence at the top of the hill. Rapid headway was made on the long run to two from home where the mare swiftly moved to the front, outjumping her rival before drawing clear in a hack canter on the run to the last. She had a good look at the crowd on the approach and was extremely slow over the fence, but she soon picked up and went on to win by an eased-down 12 lengths.

A full sister to the Fergal O'Brien-trained bumper and Listed hurdle winner Jarveys Plate, she is also a half-sister to Enda Bolger's Behind Time and closely related to point winner Incitatum.

Purchased for €155,000 by Rathmore Stud at the Goffs Punchestown Horses-In-Training Sale in May, she will now run in the colours of Kenneth Alexander who owns the likes of Honeysuckle, Edene D'arc and Minella Melody.

Like her full brother, she may be the type to improve with time and should come into her own over intermediate trips.

SPORTING JOHN
4YR BAY/BROWN GELDING

TRAINER:	Philip Hobbs
PEDIGREE:	Getaway – Wild Spell (Oscar)
FORM (P2P):	1 -
OPTIMUM TRIP:	2m 4f +
GOING:	Soft

This exciting prospect followed in the footsteps of Andy Dufresne when winning the same point-to-point at Borris House in early March and is now set to carry the famous green & gold hoops of J P McManus.

The son of Getaway faced 11 rivals and sat just off the pace for most of the three miles before making his move on the wide outside of a bunched field before the fourth from home where a good leap took him into a share of second position. Still tightly grouped, the lead changed hands at the third from home, but Jimmy O'Rourke appeared happy to hold on to his gelding who still travelled strongly on the bridle on the downhill run to the penultimate fence.

Three jumped the fence together, but on the run to the last Sporting John looked booked for second place when Jamie Codd's charge came up out of his hands to touch down with momentum. However, to this gelding's great credit, he dug deep and fought back tenaciously to get up close home to win a shade cosily on the line, recording the fastest time set on the day.

The form is extremely strong. Second home Generation Text has since joined Dan Skelton to run in the colours of Highclere Thoroughbred Racing, whilst the third, fourth and fifth went on to win next time. The form was boosted further when Hacksaw Ridge, who was pulled up, also went on to win.

You only have to take a brief look at the form of Sporting John's victory to come to the conclusion that this is an above-average individual and in today's market could look an extremely astute purchase by Kieran McManus for £160,000.

The gelding comes from a family steeped in talent. He is a half-brother to winners Kala Brandy and Kalabaloo, whilst his dam is an unraced half-sister to Lucky Baloo (dam of Oscar Whiskey). Also in the family are the likes of Seeyouatmidnight, Drumbaloo and Kahuna.

This is a horse with everything required to make the top grade. His pedigree would suggest he'll improve with time but he has the talent to win bumpers in his first season under Rules.

J P McManus – does he have another top prospect in the shape of Sporting John?

STAITHES
4YR BAY GELDING

TRAINER:	Nicky Henderson
PEDIGREE:	Watar – Corlea (Beneficial)
FORM (P2P):	1 -
OPTIMUM TRIP:	2m +
GOING:	Good to Soft

A good-looking gelding by the relatively new sire, Watar.

The Sophie Lacey-trained Staithes created a good impression on his debut in an English point-to-point at Garthorpe in late March when winning by a widening two and a half lengths from the far more experienced Signed And Sealed.

Staithes ran green in the early part of the 2m4f contest but gradually warmed to the task under Tommie O'Brien and started to make progress through the field before the fifth from home where a good leap gained him a couple of lengths. His progress continued on the run to the next where he jumped into second place before quickly bursting to the lead in the blink of an eye to hold a two-length lead on the downhill run to the next.

He guessed a little at the fence, but got away quickly and rapidly shot six or seven lengths clear before swinging wide into the home straight to face the final two. He was perhaps a little lonely out in front when steadying into the penultimate fence, but he popped over nicely and kept going with ears pricked down to the last. Again, he jumped nicely and cruised to the line without being asked too many questions.

The four-year-old left the feeling that he will improve significantly from the experience. He didn't appear to fully let himself down on the good ground and Tommie O'Brien got off and said, "He ran a bit green on the first circuit; the sun was casting a shadow on the fences. It was plain sailing after that, and the result was never in doubt."

There is not much to speak of in his immediate family, but his dam placed in bumpers and is a half-sister to Irish National third Manus The Man.

He certainly caught the eye in the parade ring at Aintree in April with his easy way of moving. He was very well turned out and looked like a proper racehorse. He now enters training with Nicky Henderson where he should win once he gathers a little experience under his belt. A softer surface may also bring out the best in him.

SWITCH HITTER
4YR BAY GELDING

TRAINER:	Paul Nicholls
PEDIGREE:	Scorpion – Country Time (Curtain Time)
FORM (P2P):	1 -
OPTIMUM TRIP:	2m +
GOING:	Good

Switch Hitter looked well above average when scoring impressively for Francesca Nimmo in an English point-to-point at Maisemore Park in April.

The attractive son of Scorpion was purchased by Francesca and her partner, former jockey Charlie Poste, for €26,000 from the Tattersalls May Sale in Ireland and made a significant return on investment when selling to Tom Malone on behalf of Paul Nicholls for £120,000 at Cheltenham's April Sale.

Expectations were high as the gelding went off a well-supported 5/4 favourite under Tommie O'Brien, who settled his mount towards the rear of mid-division in the early stages before making steady progress down the back straight where he jumped into a share of fourth position. He made a slight hash of the next (ditch) but continued to travel strongly and moved into a clear second position over the final fence down the far side before setting his sights on the long-time leader.

Ridden to improve on the long swing into the straight, the gelding quickly reduced the 10-length deficit and moved alongside Beni Light before producing a fluent leap over the penultimate fence to land with momentum. Given a shake of the reins, the bay quickly opened up his advantage before sailing over the last, allowing him to coast up the run-in to win by four and a half lengths in the fastest time set on the day.

The runner-up has subsequently franked the form twice, winning by a combined total of 118 lengths, whilst Schiap Hill, who was nine lengths back in third, also went on to win next time.

Switch Hitter is a half-brother to 2m-2m6f hurdle/chase winner Conna Cross and Frank And Honest who placed twice in point-to-points earlier this year.

This is a very nice type who looks sure to have a good career under Rules for his new connections. He will most likely gain experience in bumpers before switching to hurdles next season.

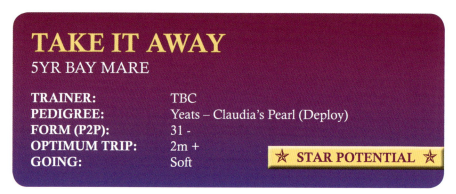

TAKE IT AWAY
5YR BAY MARE

TRAINER:	TBC
PEDIGREE:	Yeats – Claudia's Pearl (Deploy)
FORM (P2P):	31 -
OPTIMUM TRIP:	2m +
GOING:	Soft

☆ **STAR POTENTIAL** ☆

One to take seriously in the colours of J P McManus.

Take It Away did not disgrace herself when finishing third on her debut at Moig South back in March 2018, making steady headway on the final circuit to move into third position at the penultimate fence before finishing very tired in the testing conditions. Put away for the summer, the daughter of Yeats reappeared on a sounder surface at Dromahane in November where she looked a stronger, more complete model in the hands of Jamie Codd.

Waited with towards the rear in the early part of the contest, the mare edged closer as the race started to develop on the final circuit and sneaked up the inside into third place at the fifth from home. She continued to travel strongly on the heels of the leaders and came up effortlessly over the next before producing a foot-perfect leap at the third from home.

Jamie Codd still had a double handful as he produced her to lead over the penultimate fence and the pair quickened instantly on the run to the last, clearing right away in a matter of strides in the manner of a high-class individual to jump the final fence in splendid isolation before sprinting clear up the run-in to win by an impressive 12 lengths from Subtle Quest.

This truly was a scintillating performance. The form has also worked out exceptionally well with the second, third and fifth all going on to win.

Take It Away is a half-sister to Oliver Sherwood's bumper/2m3f-3m2f hurdle/useful chase winner Financial Climate. Her dam placed over 1m4f on the Flat and is a half-sister to the useful 7f/1m performer Cauvery.

Purchased by J P McManus' racing manager, Frank Berry, at the Cheltenham Sale in December for £105,000. The physically imposing daughter of Yeats has possibly taken time to come to hand.

She will be a force to be reckoned with wherever she turns up and could be very special.

NON 2021 CHELTENHAM

TELMESOMETHINGGIRL
4YR BAY FILLY

TRAINER:	TBC
PEDIGREE:	Stowaway – Wahiba Hall (Saddlers' Hall)
FORM (P2P):	1 -
OPTIMUM TRIP:	2m +
GOING:	Good to Soft

Telmesomethinggirl was possibly a fortuitous winner for trainer Colin Bowe at Ballinaboola in February, a race he had won 12 months previously with Envoi Allen.

The scopey daughter of Stowaway was one of only two mares in the seven-runner field and was given a positive ride by Barry O'Neill who positioned her prominently throughout. She momentarily dropped to fourth place at the fifth from home but continued to travel well within her comfort zone before making swift progress between horses to take up the running on the approach to the next. She continued to move well and nosed back to the front over three out before producing a foot-perfect leap at the penultimate fence where her two nearest pursuers fell independently, gifting her a healthy advantage.

She picked up readily when asked to go and win her race and popped over the last before staying on powerfully up the run-in to win by three lengths from the staying-on Zero To Hero with a further four lengths back to Minella Wizard.

Whether she would've gone on to win if the two horses had stood up at the second last is open to debate, but she appeared to have plenty left in the tank and it took her jockey plenty of time to pull her up once she had crossed the line.

She is a well-bred sort by Stowaway out of a Saddlers' Hall mare and is a half-sister to winners Mullaghanoe River and Too Many Chiefs.

Telmesomethinggirl has plenty of class and was purchased at the Cheltenham Festival Sale in March by Rathmore Stud for £150,000. I am yet to find out whom she will go into training with, but she will race in the colours of Kenneth Alexander, who owns Honeysuckle and the like.

Her pedigree suggests she will be capable of lining up in bumpers, but I fully expect her to thrive once her stamina comes into play. A sound surface may see her perform to her best.

THE BIG BREAKAWAY
4YR CHESTNUT GELDING

TRAINER:	Colin Tizzard
PEDIGREE:	Getaway – Princess Mairead (Blueprint)
FORM (P2P):	1 -
OPTIMUM TRIP:	2m 4f +
GOING:	Good to Soft

⭐ **STAR POTENTIAL** ⭐

An expensive long-term project.

Colin Tizzard likes to buy a horse with the future in mind and by the looks of it, he has the perfect model in The Big Breakaway to look forward to in years to come.

The scopey son of Getaway reportedly filled the eye in the preliminaries when well supported in the market to go off the 5/2 favourite under Rob James at Quakerstown in April.

The pair took their time as they tracked the early pace in the rear of mid-division but slowly started to make their move on the climb to the fifth from home. The gelding got in a little tight but soon recovered his ground to jump the next at the top of the hill with more fluency. Once on the level and turning the bend leading to the next, the gelding quickly latched himself on to the leaders and moved alongside before producing a big leap to take him to the front and land with a length advantage.

With momentum in his favour, he immediately established a considerable lead on the downhill section where a three-length advantage quickly doubled with another foot-perfect jump at the penultimate fence. Perhaps a little lonely out in front as he swung the bend for home, he ran a little green but popped over the last before having a good look at the crowd as he sauntered to a 10-length success in the fastest time recorded on the day.

Purchased as a foal for €17,000, he then went through the ring as a three-year-old for €55,000 before finding his way to Colin Tizzard to the tune of €360,000 at the Goffs Punchestown Sale in May.

It's a fairly hefty sum to pay, but The Big Breakaway comes from a good family which includes half-brothers For Sinead and the 156-rated Grade 3 chase winner Kildisart.

Given his imposing physique he will likely take time to fully mature, so I expect connections to not rush him this season. He looks a super long-term chaser.

Colin Tizzard – has plenty of exciting long-term prospects to look forward to

TRUCKERS PASS
5YR BROWN GELDING

TRAINER:	Philip Hobbs
PEDIGREE:	Kalanisi – Lady Knightess (Presenting)
FORM (P2P):	2 -
OPTIMUM TRIP:	2m +
GOING:	Good to Soft

Truckers Pass has a real quality to him.

The son of Kalanisi went off a very well-supported 6/4 favourite when making his debut at Ballindenisk in December 2018 and looked as if he would reward his backers when moving stylishly into contention on the exit from the back straight.

He had been held up in arrears for most of the three miles and appeared to be travelling well on the approach to the penultimate fence but forfeited his position by jumping out to his right. Once straightened up, he regained some of the lost ground and jumped the final fence as well as the leader, but didn't quite have the pace to pass him despite staying on well and pricking his ears as he crossed the line in a time which was 16 seconds quicker than the opening division.

Truckers Pass appears to have plenty of size to his frame and will have needed time to recover from what looked to be quite a gruelling race. The form has taken a few subsequent knocks but given how much ground the gelding forfeited over the second from home, he did well to finish as close as he did and looks the type to improve significantly with experience.

Originally purchased by Tom Malone acting on behalf of Paul Nicholls for £175,000, the *Racing Post* have him in training with Philip Hobbs in the colours of Brocade Racing.

He's one to keep an eye on wherever he turns up and should have a fair bit of speed being by Kalanisi out of a Presenting mare. Better ground will probably suit him.

TUCANAE
4YR BAY FILLY

TRAINER:	Anthony Black
PEDIGREE:	Yeats – Nova Cyngi (Kris S)
FORM (P2P):	1
OPTIMUM TRIP:	2m
GOING:	Good

Tucanae looks to possess a touch of class and is bred in the purple being a half-sister to top-class Queen Mother Champion Chase winner Dodging Bullets.

Handled by Richard Black, the daughter of Yeats made her debut at Dromahane in late April in a mares' maiden won by the high-class Honeysuckle 12 months ago.

She always travelled strongly up with the pace and was still hard held when jumping to the lead over three from home. She went out to her right over the next but still held a narrow advantage until Noreen Bawn challenged on her outside and hampered her on the run to the last. Momentarily knocked out of her rhythm she jumped the last a length adrift but fought back gamely all the way to the line, losing by a neck before being awarded the race.

Noreen Bawn has since sold for €220,000 at the Goffs Punchestown Sale, whilst the ninth home has since won by 10 lengths.

This filly went to the Cheltenham Sale in May but was bought back by her handler and is currently in training with Anthony Black. She may remain at the County Wexford yard, but could easily be sold privately.

Tucanae looks a strongly made mare with plenty of speed. She should have no problem competing in bumpers and has the potential to reach a decent level.

TUNE THE CHELLO
4YR BAY FILLY

TRAINER:	Henry De Bromhead
PEDIGREE:	Ask – New Cello (Orchestra)
FORM (P2P):	2 -
OPTIMUM TRIP:	2m +
GOING:	Soft

Henry De Bromhead may have a steal on his hands here after picking up Tune The Chello for £50,000.

The eye was drawn to the daughter of Ask as she made her debut in a good four-year-olds' maiden at Inch in April where she had to settle for second position despite displaying a very game attitude on the run to the line.

Tiernan Roche switched her off in the early part of the race before creeping closer at five out and produced her to challenge on the bridle at the third from home where a good jump took her into second place. Bustled along to press for the lead on the run to the next, she had around half a length to find but despite getting in a little tight to the fence, she quickened up nicely on the level and eyeballed Emtara on the run to the last. She held every chance at that point, but the eventual winner pulled out a little extra and went on to win by two lengths.

This was a gutsy performance by the runner-up who showed plenty of speed throughout the race and quickened twice to get into a challenging position.

She is related to a whole host of winners, including bumper/2m6f chase winner Team Chaser, bumper/useful 2m1f chase/2m4f hurdle winner Taking Stock, 2m3f hurdle winner Case Study and prolific 2m5f-3m3f hurdle/chase winner New Perk.

The early signs are that she will be more than capable in bumpers, but stamina is more than likely going to come to the fore as she matures.

UNBREAKABLE BOND
4YR BAY GELDING

TRAINER:	Barry Connell
PEDIGREE:	Shirocco – Caheronaun (Milan)
FORM (P2P):	2 -
OPTIMUM TRIP:	2m +
GOING:	Soft

Unbreakable Bond finished an encouraging second on his only start.

The son of Shirocco made his debut in a well-contested four-year-old geldings' maiden at Curraghmore in April where he tried to make the best of his way home when left in front at the seventh fence.

The gelding had jumped well throughout the race under Jimmy O'Rourke and showed great athleticism over the third from home to gain a couple of lengths on the field. He continued in front over the next but was joined after the last, where despite keeping on well, he didn't quite have the staying power to hold Grangeclare Native at bay on the run to the line.

By Shirocco, Unbreakable Bond may be best suited to shorter trips, although his dam was a winner over fences and hurdles up to three miles. She was closely related to Ravished, a useful 2m5f-3m1f hurdle/chase winner out of an unraced half-sister to useful bumper/2m4f-2m6f hurdle/chase winner Mount Clerigo.

Purchased by Gerry Hogan for an expensive €210,000 at the Punchestown Sale in May, he will now be owned and trained by Barry Connell who takes his trainer's licence out in the new year.

There should be plenty more to come from this gelding over shorter trips.

VANDEMERE
4YR BAY GELDING

TRAINER:	TBC
PEDIGREE:	Jeremy – Victoria Bridge (Old Vic)
FORM (P2P):	31 -
OPTIMUM TRIP:	2m
GOING:	Good

This good-moving son of Jeremy lost very little in defeat when showing a wealth of potential to finish third in a hotly contested maiden at Borris House in March on a deteriorating soft surface behind Sporting John.

He travelled eye-catchingly well in the mid-division before quickening into the lead after the fourth from home. He continued out in front over the next but after being ridden along to hold his position on the approach to the penultimate fence, he was outjumped by Generation Text and the eventual winner.

The four-year-old reappeared later that month on better ground at Portrush where he put his experience to good use and kept things simple out in front from the drop of the flag. He travelled well under Rob James who got a breather into the gelding at the halfway point before pressing on again before five out. Turning for home he quickened clear and a foot-perfect leap at the penultimate fence allowed him to carry his momentum down to the last, where again he was good before scooting up the run-in to win by a commanding seven lengths.

By Jeremy, he is a half-brother to 2m hurdle/2m3f chase winner At Your Ease. His dam is an unraced half-sister to 2m4f and 2m5f hurdle winner Likearollingstone out of a half-sister to high-class staying hurdle Bannow Bay.

Sold as a foal for €18,500, he went on to make €50,000 as a three-year-old before fetching £120,000 at Aintree in April when selling to Seamus Burns.

Vandemere is not the biggest but his athletic forward way of moving will stand him in good stead in bumpers before being sent over hurdles.

WHO'S THE BOSS
4YR BAY/BROWN FILLY

TRAINER:	Stuart Edmunds
PEDIGREE:	Oscar – Final Episode (Definite Article)
FORM (P2P):	2 -
OPTIMUM TRIP:	2m +
GOING:	Soft

Who's The Boss made her debut at Monksgrange in a highly competitive mares' maiden for trainer Mary Doyle in the colours of Baltimore Stables at the end of March where she made a lasting impression despite finishing second.

The bonny-looking daughter of Oscar was ridden patiently towards the rear for most of the three miles under Harley Dunne, before making stealthy progress after taking the fourth from home. The pair continued to make ground on the run to the next and moved into third position upon touching down before gaining a further place on the uphill section of the track. Rounding the bend for home the tempo increased significantly as she moved alongside the eventual winner and the pair were locked together over the penultimate fence. Toe-to-toe on the run to the last, Who's The Boss ran around slightly but jumped well before sticking her neck out gamely all the way up the straight, only to be denied by a head.

This race had a strong look to it. The Colin Bowe-trained winner has since been purchased for £115,000 by Tom Malone and Paul Nicholls whilst the fourth went on to be a runner-up next time and is now with Lucinda Russell. The fifth won by seven lengths on her next start and is now with Donald McCain and the sixth was a solid third in another competitive mares' maiden next time.

Bought for £60,000 by J D Moore at the Goffs Aintree Sale in April, she now enters training with Stuart Edmunds who has great success with the horses who come his way.

She's not the biggest individual, but what she lacks in size, she makes up for in heart and should be more than capable in a bumper. By Oscar, she may also appreciate a little give underfoot.

WIDE RECEIVER
4YR BAY GELDING

TRAINER:	Gordon Elliott
PEDIGREE:	Sholokhov – Sagarich (Sagamix)
FORM (P2P):	1 -
OPTIMUM TRIP:	2m +
GOING:	Soft

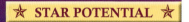

★ STAR POTENTIAL ★

Wide Receiver has the potential to develop into a leading bumper candidate.

The Cormac Farrell-trained gelding was the joint outsider when making his debut in a five-runner four-year-olds' maiden at Cragmore over the intermediate trip of 2m4f in February where he clearly demonstrated he was head and shoulders above the field when bounding to an effortless success.

The son of Sholokhov always caught the eye going well as he sat just off the heels of the pacesetters before producing a spring-heeled leap at the fourth from home where he moved into a share of the lead. He continued to go toe-to-toe with Thechaseison on the run to the next and produced a more efficient jump to touch down with a narrow advantage, which he increased handsomely for gentle pressure, readily quickening clear on the long uphill section of the track.

He soon opened up a six-or seven-length break on the field as he galloped on remorselessly to the penultimate fence, where although he didn't get very high, he landed unscathed and extended further clear after Simon Cavanagh became more vigorous in the saddle. He was much better over the last and scooted up the run-in to win by an impressive eight lengths with a further six back to the third.

The form has taken a couple of subsequent knocks but it's impossible not to be impressed with how this gelding picked up when asked the question by his jockey. I loved the way he grabbed the ground and used his front shoulders to gain speed and momentum. It's open to suggestion just how good he could turn out to be, but Tom Malone acting on behalf of Gordon Elliott outbid Harold Kirk to the tune of £410,000 at the Cheltenham Sale in February.

By Sholokhov (sire of Don Cossack) out of a Sagamix mare, he is a half-brother to Denis Hogan's Young Dev who won over three miles on heavy ground and was also placed in bumpers. His dam won over 1m4f on the Flat for Charlie Swan before winning a 2m1f novices' hurdle contest for Michael Quinlan. She is a half-sister to a 1m7f and 15.5f Listed winner on the Flat who later went on to score at the same level over hurdles.

This is a pedigree littered with both speed and stamina and judging by this gelding's electric turn of foot he could quite easily make his presence felt in bumpers before being stepped up in trip later in his career.

Gordon Elliott – should have plenty more reasons to celebrate

YOUNG BUCK
5YR BAY GELDING

TRAINER:	Paul Nicholls
PEDIGREE:	Yeats – Pepsi Starlet (Heavenly Manna)
FORM (P2P):	1 -
OPTIMUM TRIP:	2m 4f +
GOING:	Soft

A proper staying performance saw this likeable individual make a winning debut.

Young Buck burst on to the scene in a five-year-old geldings' maiden at Nenagh in February and clearly knew his job as he bounced out to make all the running when the flags went up, clocking the fastest time set on the day.

Trained by John 'Shark' Hanlon and ridden by the excellent Tom Hamilton, the son of Yeats travelled well at the head of affairs and held a comfortable two-length advantage as he jumped four from home. The field were well spaced out by the time they reached the next and following the departure of Half Shot, the gelding had only the ridden along Jack Hackett for company.

The pair were virtually stride for stride as they pulled 15 lengths clear of the remainder, but Young Buck was still hard on the bridle and gradually eased ahead on the uphill run to the penultimate fence which he jumped neatly before extending his advantage on the run to the last. Kept up to his work on the tiring climb, the gelding pricked his ears on the approach to the fence but made a bad mistake before being picked up to gallop through the line with five lengths to spare over Jack Hackett, with a further 12 lengths back to the third.

This was a very likeable performance from the front for a debutant. The two-furlong climb to the line takes some getting and despite taking a chance at the last the gelding had plenty left in the locker to carry on to the line.

Sold as a foal for €30,000, he then went to the Goffs Land Rover Sale as a three-year-old and made €36,000 before achieving a good return on investment when selling to Paul Nicholls for £150,000 at the Cheltenham Festival earlier this year.

The five-year-old comes from a good family. His dam has produced seven winners from nine runners, including the useful 2m1f chase/2m6f chase winner Queens Wild, useful 2m4f chaser The Phantom Piper and 2m5f-2m7f chaser Caspian Piper. The latest winner from the family is Dan Skelton's I'm Always Trying who won a 3m2f hurdle contest at Fontwell in July 2018.

Given his age I would imagine connections will want to crack on over hurdles where I would imagine he will excel when the emphasis is on stamina. His knee action also suggests a softer surface will see him at his best.

Index

Star Potential Horses appear in purple

ADRIMEL	*5*
ASK A HONEY BEE	6
BALLINSKER	7
BAPTISM OF FIRE	9
BARBADOS BUCK'S	10
BELLA BALLERINA	*11*
BIG BRESIL	*12*
BLEUE AWAY	13
BLOSSOMING FORTH	*14*
BOBHOPEORNOHOPE	15
BOLD ASSASSIN	16
BOLD CONDUCT	*18*
BRAVEMANSGAME	19
BRIEF AMBITION	*20*
BROKEN HALO	22
CAPTAIN BLACKPEARL	*23*
CARRY ON THE MAGIC	24
CILL ANNA	25
CLONDAW CAITLIN	26
DEFUTURE IS BRIGHT	27
DEPLOY THE GETAWAY	*28*
DIRECT FIRE	29
DO THE FLOSS	30
DOES HE KNOW	31
ECLAIR ON LINE	32
ECLAIR SURF	33

EMTARA	*34*
ESCARIA TEN	***35***
EVANDER	*36*
EXOD'ELA	*37*
FADO DES BROSSES	*39*
FAROUK D'ALENE	***40***
FERNY HOLLOW	***41***
FILOU DES ISSARDS	*43*
GABBYS CROSS	*44*
GENERATION TEXT	*45*
GERALDO	*46*
GETAWAY PAT	***47***
GIANTS TABLE	*48*
GLYNN	*49*
GRANDADS COTTAGE	*50*
GRANGECLARE NATIVE	*51*
GUNSIGHT RIDGE	*52*
HEARTBREAK KID	*53*
HOLD THAT TAUGHT	***54***
IDAS BOY	*55*
IMPERIAL FLEM	*56*
IN TOO DEEP	*58*
ISRAEL CHAMP	***59***
IT SURE IS	*60*
JANUARY JETS	***61***
JAVA POINT	*63*
JEREMY PASS	*64*
KAKAMORA	*65*
KID COMMANDO	***66***

LARGY FIX	**67**
LETS GO CHAMP	68
LINELEE KING	**69**
LOOK ALIVE	70
MADERA MIST	71
MAKE ME A BELIEVER	73
MEYER LANSKY	74
MINELLA TARA	75
MINELLA TRUMP	76
MOORE CLOUDS	77
MOSSY FEN	78
MUSTANG ALPHA	79
MY WHIRLWIND	**80**
NOREEN BAWN	**81**
OFFTHESHOULDER	82
ON THE BANDWAGON	83
PAPA TANGO CHARLY	**85**
PENS MAN	86
PICANHA	87
POWER OF PAUSE	88
RAMILLIES	89
RIVER TYNE	90
ROYAL CROWN	91
SKATMAN	92
SOUTHERN GIRL	**93**
SPORTING JOHN	94
STAITHES	96
SWITCH HITTER	97
TAKE IT AWAY	**98**
TELMESOMETHINGGIRL	99

THE BIG BREAKAWAY   *100*   NO More

TRUCKERS PASS   *102*

TUCANAE   *103*

TUNE THE CHELLO   *104*

UNBREAKABLE BOND   *105*

VANDEMERE   *106*

WHO'S THE BOSS   *107*

WIDE RECEIVER   *108*

YOUNG BUCK   *110*

Bellurgan Park

Coming down the hill at Oldtown

Watching on